MY CHILDREN!
MY AFRICA!

BOOKS BY ATHOL FUGARD
AVAILABLE FROM TCG

A Lesson From Aloes
Notebooks: 1960–1977
The Road to Mecca
Statements

FORTHCOMING
Blood Knot & Other Plays

ATHOL
FUGARD

MY CHILDREN!
MY AFRICA!

THEATRE COMMUNICATIONS GROUP

This publication is made possible in part with public funds from the New York State Council on the Arts, a State Agency.

TCG books are exclusively distributed to the book trade by Consortium Book Sales and Distribution, 1045 Westgate Drive, St. Paul, MN 55114.

Cover: John Kani in the New York Theatre Workshop production of *My Children! My Africa!* Frontis: Courtney Vance and Lisa Fugard. All photographs copyright 1989 by Gerry Goodstein.

Fugard, Athol.
My children! My Africa! / by Athol Fugard.
ISBN-13: 978-1-55936-014-2
ISBN-10: 1-55936-014-3
I. Title.
PR9639.3F8M9   1990   90-11252
822—dc20   CIP

Design and composition by The Sarabande Press

First Edition, October 1990
Seventh Printing, January 2005

For Lisa and John

My Children! My Africa! was first presented in the United States by the New York Theatre Workshop on December 18, 1989, under the direction of the playwright. Set and costume design was by Susan Hilferty, lighting design by Dennis Parichy, and sound design by Mark Bennett. The cast was as follows:

Mr. M (Anela Myalatya)	*John Kani*
Isabel Dyson	*Lisa Fugard*
Thami Mbikwana	*Courtney B. Vance*

The play was originally produced by The Market Theatre, Johannesburg, June 1989.

MY CHILDREN!
MY AFRICA!

MR. M (ANELA MYALATYA)

ISABEL DYSON

THAMI MBIKWANA

TIME AND PLACE

The action takes place in a small Eastern Cape Karoo town in the autumn of 1984.

ACT
ONE

◆

SCENE 1

Classroom of the Zolile High School. Mr. M is at a table with Thami and Isabel on either side of him. A lively interschool debate is in progress. Everybody is speaking at the same time.

MR. M: Order please!

ISABEL: I never said anything of the kind.

THAMI: Yes you did. You said that women were more—

MR. M: I call you both to order!

ISABEL: What I said was that women—

THAMI: —were more emotional than men—

ISABEL: Correction! That women were more intuitive than men—

MR. M: Miss Dyson and Mr. Mbikwana! Will you both
please —
ISABEL: You are twisting my words and misquoting me.
THAMI: I am not. I am simply asking you —
MR. M: Come to order!

Grabs the school bell and rings it violently. This works. Silence.

I think it is necessary for me to remind all of you exactly
what a debate is supposed to be.
*(Opens and reads from a little black dictionary that is at
hand on the table)* My dictionary defines it as follows: "The
orderly and regulated discussion of an issue with opposing
viewpoints receiving equal time and consideration."
Shouting down the opposition so that they cannot be
heard does not comply with that definition.

Enthusiasm for your cause is most commendable but
without personal discipline it is as useless as having a good
donkey and a good cart but no harness.

We are now running out of time. I am therefore closing
the open section of our debate. No more interruptions
from the floor please. We'll bring our proceedings to a
close with a brief, I repeat *brief,* three minutes at the
most, summing up of our arguments.

Starting with the proposers of the motion: Mr. Thami
Mbikwana of the Zolile High School, will you please make
your concluding statement.

*Thami stands up. Wild round of applause from the audience. He
is secure and at ease. He is speaking to an audience of
schoolmates. His "concluding statement" is outrageous and he
knows it and enjoys it.*

THAMI: I don't stand here now and speak to you as your friend
and schoolmate. That would lessen the seriousness of my
words to you. No! Close your eyes, forget that you know

2

my face and voice, forget that you know anything about
Thami Mbikwana. Think of me rather as an oracle, of my
words as those of the great ancestors of our traditional
African culture, which we turn our back on and desert to
our great peril!

The opposition has spoken about sexual exploitation and
the need for women's liberation. Brothers and sisters these
are foreign ideas. Do not listen to them. They come from
a culture, the so-called Western Civilization, that has
meant only misery to Africa and its people. It is the same
culture that shipped away thousands of our ancestors as
slaves, the same culture that has exploited Africa with the
greed of a vulture during the period of Colonialism and
the same culture which continues to exploit us in the
twentieth century under the disguise of concern for our
future.

The opposition has not been able to refute my claim
that women cannot do the same jobs as men because they
are not the equals of us physically and that a woman's role
in the family, in society is totally different to that of a
man's. These facts taken together reinforce what our
fathers, and our grandfathers and our great-grandfathers
knew; namely that happiness and prosperity for the tribe
and the nation is achieved when education of the little
ladies takes these facts into consideration. Would it be
right for a woman to go to war while the man sits at the
sewing machine? I do not have milk in my breasts to feed
the baby while my wife is out digging up roads for the
Divisional Council.

Wild laughter.

Brothers and sisters, it is obvious that you feel the same as
I do about this most serious matter. I hope that at the end

of this debate, your vote will reflect your agreement with me.

Wild applause and whistles.

MR. M: Thank you Mr. Mbikwana.

Thami sits.

And now finally, a last statement from the captain of the visiting team, Miss Isabel Dyson of Camdeboo Girls High.

Polite applause. Isabel stands. She takes on the audience with direct unflinching eye contact. She is determined not to be intimidated.

ISABEL: You have had to listen to a lot of talk this afternoon about traditional values, traditional society, your great ancestors, your glorious past. In spite of what has been implied I want to start off by telling you that I have as much respect and admiration for your history and tradition as anybody else. I believe most strongly that there are values and principles in traditional African society which could be studied with great profit by the Western Civilization so scornfully rejected by the previous speaker. But at the same time, I know, and you know, that Africa no longer lives in that past. For better or for worse it is part now of the twentieth century and all the nations on this continent are struggling very hard to come to terms with that reality. Arguments about sacred traditional values, the traditional way of life et cetera and et cetera, are used by those who would like to hold back Africa's progress and keep it locked up in the past.

Maybe there was a time in the past when a woman's life consisted of bearing children and hoeing the fields while men sharpened their spears and sat around waiting for

4

another war to start. But it is a silly argument that relies on that old image of primitive Africa for its strength. It is an argument that insults your intelligence. Times have changed. Sheer brute strength is not the determining factor anymore. You do not need the muscles of a prize fighter when you sit down to operate the computers that control today's world. The American space program now has women astronauts on board the space shuttles doing the same jobs as men. As for the difference in the emotional and intellectual qualities of men and women, remember that it is a question of difference and not inferiority and that with those differences go strengths which compensate for weaknesses in the opposite sex.

And lastly, a word of warning. The argument against equality for women, in education or any other field, based on alleged "differences" between the two sexes, is an argument that can very easily be used against any other "different" group. It is an argument based on prejudice, not fact. I ask you not to give it your support. Thank you.

She sits. Polite applause.

MR. M: Thank you Miss Dyson. We come now to the vote. But before we do that, a word of caution. We have had a wonderful experience this afternoon. Don't let it end on a frivolous and irresponsible note. Serious issues have been debated. Vote accordingly. To borrow a phrase from Mr. Mbikwana, forget the faces, remember the words. If you believe that we have the right to vote out there in the big world, then show here, in the classroom, that you know how to use it.

We'll take it on a count of hands, and for the benefit of any over-enthusiastic supporters, only one hand per person please. Let me read the proposal once again: "That in view

of the essential physical and psychological differences between men and women, there should be correspondingly different educational syllabuses for the two sexes."
    All those in favor raise a hand.

Mr. M, Thami and Isabel count hands.

Seventeen?

Thami and Isabel nod agreement.

All those against.

They all count again.

Twenty-four?

Reactions from Thami and Isabel.

The proposal is defeated by twenty-four votes to seventeen. Before we break just a reminder about the special choir practice this afternoon. Members of the choir must please join Mrs. Magada in Number Two Classroom after school. *(To Isabel and Thami)* Allow me to offer you my congratulations Miss Dyson on a most well-deserved victory. What do you say Mbikwana?

THAMI *(To Isabel)*: Your concluding statement was a knockout.

MR. M: You didn't do too badly yourself.

ISABEL: You made me so angry!

THAMI *(All innocence)*: I did?

ISABEL: *Ja* you did. *(Thami laughs)* I was beginning to think you actually believed what you were saying.

THAMI: But I do!

ISABEL: Oh, come on . . . !

MR. M *(Rubbing his hands with pleasure)*: All I can say is . . . Splendid! Splendid! Splendid! The intellect in action. Challenge and response. That is what a good debate is all about. And whatever you do young lady, don't

6

underestimate your achievement in winning the popular vote. It wasn't easy for that audience to vote against Mbikwana. He's one of them, and a very popular "one of them" I might add. *(Waving a finger at Thami)* You were quite shameless in the way you tried to exploit that loyalty.

THAMI *(Another laugh)*: Was that wrong?

MR. M: No. As the saying goes, all is fair in love, war and debating. But the fact that you didn't succeed is what makes me really happy. I am very proud of our audience. In my humble opinion they are the real winners this afternoon. You two just had to talk and argue. Anybody can do that. They had to listen . . . intelligently!

ISABEL: They certainly gave me a good time.

MR. M: That was very apparent, if I may say so Miss Dyson. I can't thank you enough for coming to us today. I sincerely hope there'll be another occasion.

ISABEL: Same here.

MR. M: Good! *(Consults his watch)* Now you must excuse me. There is a staff meeting waiting for me. Will you look after Miss Dyson please Mbikwana?

THAMI: Yes teacher.

Mr. M leaves. Isabel and Thami pack away into their bookbags the papers and books they used in the debate. Without the mediating presence of Mr. M they are both a little self-conscious. First moves in the ensuing conversation are awkward.

ISABEL: I wish we had a teacher like . . . Mr. . . . . *(Pronouncing the name carefully)* M-ya-lat-ya. Did I say it right?

THAMI: Yes you did, but nobody calls him that. He's just plain Mr. M to everybody.

ISABEL: Mr. M.

THAMI: That's right.

ISABEL: Well I think he's wonderful.

THAMI: He's okay.

ISABEL: I had a geography teacher in Standard Seven who was a little bit like him. Full of fun and lots of energy.

THAMI: *Ja*, that's Mr. M all right.

Pause.

ISABEL: I meant what I said to him. I really did have a good time.

THAMI: Same here.

ISABEL: You did? Because to be honest with you, I wasn't expecting it.

THAMI: Me neither.

ISABEL: No?

THAMI: Nope.

ISABEL: Why not?

THAMI *(Embarrassed)*: Well . . . you know . . .

ISABEL: Let me guess. You've never debated with girls before.

He nods, smiling sheepishly.

And white girls at that! I don't believe it. You boys are all the same.

THAMI: But you were good!

ISABEL: Because I happen to feel very strongly about what we were debating. But it was also the whole atmosphere you know. It was so . . . so free and easy. The debates at my school are such stuffy affairs. And so boring most of the time. Everything is done according to the rules with everybody being polite and nobody getting excited . . . lots of discipline but very little enthusiasm. This one was a riot!

THAMI *(Finger to his lips)*: Be careful.

ISABEL: Of what?

THAMI: That word.

ISABEL: Which one?

THAMI: Riot! Don't say it in a black township. Police start shooting as soon as they hear it.

ISABEL: Oh. I'm sorry.

THAMI (*Having a good laugh*): It's a joke Isabel.

ISABEL: Oh . . . you caught me off guard. I didn't think you would joke about those things.

THAMI: Riots and police? Oh yes, we joke about them. We joke about everything.

ISABEL: Okay, then I'll say it again: this afternoon was a riot.

THAMI: Good! Try that one on your folks when you get home tonight. Say the newspapers have got it all wrong. You had a wonderful time taking part in a little township riot.

This time Isabel does get the joke. A good laugh.

ISABEL: Oh *ja*, I can just see my mom and dad cracking up at that one.

THAMI: They wouldn't think it was funny? (*The idea of whites reacting to township humor amuses him enormously*)

ISABEL: Are you kidding? They even take the Marx Brothers seriously. I can just hear my mom: "Isabel, I think it is very wrong to joke about those things!"

THAMI: Dyson! That's an English name.

ISABEL: Sober, sensible, English-speaking South African. I'm the third generation.

THAMI: What does your dad do?

ISABEL: He's a chemist. The chemist shop in town. Karoo Pharmacy. That's ours. My mother and sister work in it as well, and on Saturdays, provided there isn't a hockey match, so do I.

THAMI: Any brothers?

ISABEL: No. Just the four of us.

THAMI: A happy family.

ISABEL: *Ja*, I suppose you could call us that. Mind you, Lucille would say it would be a lot happier if only her little sister would be, as she puts it, "more accommodating of others."

THAMI: What does she mean?

ISABEL: She means she doesn't like the fact that I've got opinions of my own. I'm the rebel in the family.

THAMI: That sounds interesting.

ISABEL: I can't help it. Whenever it's time for a family *indaba* . . . you know, when we sit down in the living room to discuss family business and things . . . I just always seem to end up disagreeing with everybody and wanting to do things differently.

But other than that, *ja*, an average sort of happy family. What else do you want to know. Go ahead, anything . . . provided I also get a turn to ask questions.

Thami studies her.

Eighteen years old. I think I want to be a writer. My favorite subject is English and my favorite sport, as you might have guessed, is hockey. Anything else?

THAMI: Yes. What did you have for breakfast this morning?

ISABEL: Auntie, our maid, put down in front of me a plate of steaming, delicious jungle oats over which I sprinkled a crust of golden brown sugar, and while that was melting on top I added a little moat of chilled milk all around the side. That was followed by brown-bread toast, quince jam and lots and lots of tea.

THAMI: Yes, you're a writer.

ISABEL: You think so?

THAMI: You made me hungry.

ISABEL: My turn now?

THAMI: Yep.

ISABEL: Let's start with your family.

THAMI: Mbikwana! *(He clears his throat)* Mbikwana is an old
Bantu name and my mother and my father are good,
reliable, ordinary, hardworking Bantu-speaking black
South African natives. I am the one-hundred-thousandth
generation.

ISABEL: You really like teasing, don't you.

THAMI: Amos and Lilian Mbikwana. They're in Cape Town.
My mother is a domestic and my father works for the
railways. I stay here with my grandmother and married
sister. I was sent to school in the peaceful *platteland*
because it is so much safer you see than the big city with
all its temptations and troubles. *(He laughs)* Another Bantu
joke.

ISABEL: You're impossible!

*They are now beginning to relax with each other. Isabel finds the
class register on the desk.*

"Zolile High School. Standard Ten." *(She opens it and reads)*
Awu.

THAMI *(Pointing to the appropriate desk in the classroom)*: There.
Johnny. Center forward in our soccer team.

ISABEL: Bandla.

THAMI: There.

ISABEL: Cwati.

THAMI: Cwati. There.

ISABEL: Who was the chap sitting there who laughed at *all*
your jokes and applauded *everything* you said.

THAMI: Stephen Gaika. He's mad!

ISABEL: And your best friend?

THAMI: They are all my friends.

ISABEL: And where does . . . *(She finds his name in the register)*
Thami Mbikwana sit?

Thami points. Isabel goes to the desk and sits.

THAMI: Yes that's the one. For nearly two years I've sat there
. . . being educated!

ISABEL *(Reading names carved into the wood of the desk)*: John,
Bobby, Zola, Bo . . . Boni . . .

THAMI: Bonisile.

ISABEL: Where's your name?

THAMI: You won't find it there. I don't want to leave any part
of me in this classroom.

ISABEL: That sounds heavy.

THAMI: It's been heavy. You've got no problems with it, hey.

ISABEL: With school? No not really. Couple of teachers have
tried their best to spoil it for me, but they haven't
succeeded. I've had a pretty good time in fact. I think I
might even end up with the old cliché . . . you know,
school years, best years, happiest years . . . whatever it is
they say.

THAMI: No. I won't be saying that.

ISABEL: That surprises me.

THAMI: Why?

ISABEL: *Ja*, come on, wouldn't you be if I said it? You're
obviously clever. I'll bet you sail through your exams.

THAMI: It's not as simple as just passing exams, Isabel. School
doesn't mean the same to us that it does to you.

ISABEL: Go on.

THAMI: I used to like it. Junior school? You should have seen
me. I wanted to have school on Saturdays and Sundays as
well. Yes, I did. Other boys wanted to kill me. I hated
the holidays.

ISABEL: So what happened?

THAMI: I changed.

ISABEL: *Ja*, I'm listening.

THAMI *(A shrug)*: That's all. I changed. Things changed.
Everything changed.

ISABEL *(Realizing she is not going to get any more out of him)*: Only five months to go.

THAMI: I'm counting.

ISABEL: What then?

THAMI: After school? *(Another shrug)* I don't know yet. Do you?

ISABEL: *Ja.* Rhodes University. I want to study journalism.

THAMI: Newspaper reporter.

ISABEL: And radio, TV. It's a very wide field now. You can specialize in all sorts of things. *(Perplexed)* Don't you want to study further Thami?

THAMI: I told you, I'm not sure about anything yet.

ISABEL: What does Mr. M say?

THAMI: It's got nothing to do with him.

ISABEL: But you're his favorite, aren't you?

Noncommittal shrug from Thami.

I bet you are. And I also bet you anything you like that he's got a career planned out for you.

THAMI *(Sharply)*: What I do with my life has got nothing to do with him.

ISABEL: Sorry.

THAMI: I don't listen to what he says and I don't do what he says.

ISABEL: I said I'm sorry, I didn't mean to interfere.

THAMI: That's all right. It's just that he makes me so mad sometimes. He always thinks *he* knows what is best for me. He never asks me how I feel about things. I know he means well, but I'm not a child anymore. I've got ideas of my own now.

ISABEL *(Placating)*: *Ja,* I know what you mean. I've had them in my life as well. They always know what is best for you, don't they. So anyway, listen . . . I'm going to write up the debate for our school newspaper. I'll send you a copy if you like.

THAMI: You got a school newspaper! How about that!

ISABEL: It's a bit unethical reporting on a contest in which I took part, and won, but I promise to be objective. I made notes of most of your main points.

THAMI: You can have my speech if you want it.

ISABEL: Hell, thanks. That will make it much easier . . . and guarantee there won't be any misquotes!

Thami hands over the speech. It is obvious that they both want to prolong the conversation, but this is prevented by the sound of Mr. M's bell being rung vigorously in the distance. They check wristwatches.

ISABEL: Oh my God, look at the time!

They grab their bookbags and run.

SCENE 2

Isabel alone. She speaks directly to the audience.

ISABEL: It's on the edge of town, on the right-hand side when you drive out to join the National Road going north to Middleberg. Unfortunately, as most of Camdeboo would say, you can't miss it. I discovered the other day that it has actually got a name . . . Brakwater . . . from the old farm that used to be there. Now everybody just calls it "the location." There's been a lot of talk lately about moving it to where it can't be seen. Our mayor, Mr. Pienaar, was in our shop the other day and I heard him say to my dad that it was "very much to be regretted" that the first thing that greeted any visitor to the town was the "terrible mess of the location." To be fair to old

Pienaar he has got a point you know. Our town is very pretty. We've got a lot of nicely restored National Monument houses and buildings. Specially in the Main Street. Our shop is one of them. The location is quite an eyesore by comparison. Most of the houses—if you can call them that!—are made of bits of old corrugated iron or anything else they could find to make four walls and a roof. There are no gardens or anything like that. You've got to drive in first gear all the time because of the potholes and stones, and when the wind is blowing and all the dust and rubbish flying around . . . ! I think you'd be inclined to agree with our mayor.

I've actually been into it quite a few times. With my mom to visit Auntie, our maid, when she was sick. And with my dad when he had to take emergency medicines to the clinic. I can remember one visit, just sitting in the car and staring out of the window trying to imagine what it would be like to live my whole life in one of those little *pondoks*. No electricity, no running water, no privacy! Auntie's little house has only got two small rooms and nine of them sleep there. I ended up being damn glad I was born with a white skin.

But don't get the wrong idea. I'm not saying I've spent a lot of time thinking about it seriously or anything like that.

It's just been there, you know, on the edge of my life, the way it is out there on the edge of town. So when Miss Brockway, our principal, called me in and told me that the black school had started a debating society and had invited us over for a debate, I didn't have any objections. She said it was a chance for a "pioneering intellectual exchange" between the two schools.

She also said she had checked with the police and they had said it would be all right provided we were driven straight to the school and then straight out afterwards. There's been a bit of trouble in the location again and people are starting to get nervous about it. So off we went . . . myself, Renee Vermaas and Cathy Bullard, the C.G.H. Debating Team . . . feeling very virtuous about our "pioneering" mission into the location. As Renee tactfully put it: "Shame! We must remember that English isn't their home language. So don't use too many big words and speak slowly and carefully."

They were waiting for us in what they called Number One Classroom. *(Shaking her head)* Honestly, I would rate it as the most bleak, depressing, dingy classroom I have ever been in. Everything about it was gray—the cement floor, the walls, the ceiling. When I first saw it I thought to myself, how in God's name does anybody study or learn anything in here. But there they were, about forty of them, my age, mostly boys, not one welcoming smile among the lot of them. And they *were* studying something and very intently . . . three privileged and uncomfortable white girls, in smart uniforms, from a posh school, who had come to give them a lesson in debating. I know I'm a good debater and one of the reasons for that is that I always talk very directly to the audience and the opposition. I am not shy about making eye contact. Well, when I did it this time, when it was my turn to speak and I stood up and looked at those forty unsmiling faces, I suddenly realized that I hadn't prepared myself for one simple but all-important fact: they had no intention of being grateful to me. They were sitting there waiting to judge me, what I said and how I said it, on the basis of total equality. Maybe it doesn't sound like such a big thing to you, but you must understand I had never really confronted that before, and I don't just mean in debates. I mean in my life!

I'm not saying I've had no contact across the color line.
Good heavens no! I get as much of that as any average
young white South African. I have a great time every
morning with Auntie in the kitchen when she's cooking
breakfast and we gossip about everything and everybody
in town. And then there's Samuel with his crash helmet
and scooter . . . he delivers medicines for my dad . . . I
have wonderful long conversations with him about religion
and the meaning of life generally. He's a very staunch
Zionist. Church every Sunday. But it's always "Miss
Isabel," the *baas*'s daughter, that he's talking to. When I
stood up in front of those black matric pupils in Number
One Classroom it was a very different story. I wasn't at
home or in my dad's shop or in my school or any of the
other safe places in my life.

I was in Brakwater! It was *their* school. It was *their*
world. I was the outsider and I was being asked to prove
myself. Standing there in front of them like that I felt
. . . exposed! . . . in a way that has never happened to
me before. Cathy told me afterwards that she's never heard
me start a debate *so* badly and finish it *so* strongly.

God, it was good! I don't know when exactly it
happened, but about halfway through my opening
address, I realized that everything about that moment
. . . the miserable little classroom, myself, my voice,
what I was saying and them hearing and understanding
me, because I knew they understood me—they were
staring and listening so hard I could feel it on my skin!—
all of it had become one of the most real experiences I
have ever had. I have never before had so . . . so exciting
. . . a sense of myself! Because that *is* what we all want,
isn't it? For things to be real, our lives, our thoughts,
what we say and do? That's what I want, now. I didn't
really know it before that debate, but I do now. You see I

finally worked out what happened to me in the classroom.
I discovered a new world! I've always thought about the
location as just a sort of embarrassing backyard to our neat
and proper little white world, where our maids and our
gardeners and our delivery boys went at the end of the
day. But it's not. It's a whole world of its own with its
own life that has nothing to do with us. If you put
together all the Brakwaters in the country, then it's a
pretty big one—and if you'll excuse my language—there's
a hell of a lot of people living in it! That's quite a
discovery you know. But it's also a little—what's the
word?—disconcerting! You see, it means that what I
thought was out there for me . . . no! it's worse than that!
it's what I was made to believe was out there for me . . .
the ideas, the chances, the people . . . specially the
people! . . . all of that is only a small fraction of what it
could be.

(*Shaking her head*) No. Or as Auntie says in the kitchen
when she's not happy about something: *Aikona!* Not good
enough. I'm greedy. I want more. I want as much as I can
get.

SCENE 3

*Isabel alone. Mr. M enters, hat in hand, mopping his brow with
a handkerchief.*

MR. M: Miss Dyson! There you are.
ISABEL (*Surprised*): Hello!
MR. M: My apologies for descending on you out of the blue
like this but I've been looking for you high and low. One
of your schoolmates said I would find you here.

ISABEL: Don't apologize. It's a pleasure to see you again Mr.
M.

MR. M *(Delighted)*: Mr. M! How wonderful to hear you call me
that.

ISABEL: You must blame Thami for my familiarity.

MR. M: Blame him? On the contrary, I will thank him most
gratefully. Hearing you call me Mr. M like all the others
at the school gives me a happy feeling that you are also a
member of my very extended family.

ISABEL: I'd like to be.

MR. M: Then welcome to my family Miss . . .

ISABEL *(Before he can say it)*: "Isabel" if you please Mr. M, just
plain "Isabel."

MR. M *(Bowing)*: Then doubly welcome young Isabel.

ISABEL *(Curtsy)*: I thank you kind sir.

MR. M: You have great charm young lady. I can understand
now how you managed to leave so many friends behind
you after only one visit to the school. Hardly a day passes
without someone stopping me and asking: When is Isabel
Dyson and her team coming back?

ISABEL: Well? When are we?

MR. M: You would still welcome a return visit?

ISABEL: But of course.

MR. M: Why so emphatically "of course"?

ISABEL: Because I enjoyed the first one so emphatically very
much.

MR. M: The unruly behavior of my young family wasn't too
much for you?

ISABEL: Didn't I also get a little unruly once or twice, Mr. M?

MR. M: Yes, now that you mention it. You certainly gave as
good as you got.

ISABEL *(With relish)*: And that is precisely why I enjoyed
myself . . .

MR. M: You like a good fight.

ISABEL: *Ja.* Specially the ones I win!

MR. M: Splendid! Splendid! Splendid! Because that is precisely what I have come to offer you.

ISABEL: Your Thami wants a return bout, does he?

MR. M: He will certainly welcome the opportunity to salvage his pride when it comes along . . . his friends are teasing him mercilessly . . . but what I have come to talk to you about is a prospect even more exciting than that. I have just seen Miss Brockway and she has given it her official blessing. It was her suggestion that I approach you directly. So here I am. Can you spare a few minutes?

ISABEL: As many as you like.

MR. M: It came to me as I sat there in Number One trying to be an impartial referee while you and Thami went for each other hammer and tongs, no holds barred and no quarter given or asked. I don't blame our audience for being so unruly. Once or twice I felt like doing some shouting myself. What a contest! But at the same time, what a waste I thought! Yes you heard me correctly. A waste! They shouldn't be fighting each other. They should be fighting together! If the sight of them as opponents is so exciting, imagine what it would be like if they were allies. If those two stood side by side and joined forces, they could take on anybody . . . and win! For the next few days that is all I could think of. It tormented me. When I wrote my report about the debate in the school diary, that was the last sentence. "But oh!, what a waste!"

The truth is, I've seen too much of it Isabel. Wasted people! Wasted chances! It's become a phobia with me now. It's not easy you know to be a teacher, to put your heart and soul into educating an eager young mind which you know will never get a chance to develop further and realize its full potential. The thought that you and Thami would be another two victims of this country's lunacy, was almost too much for me.

The time for lamentations is passed. *(Takes an envelope from his pocket)* Two days ago I received this in the mail. It's the program for this year's Grahamstown Schools Festival. It has given me what I was looking for . . . an opportunity to fight the lunacy. The Standard Bank is sponsoring a new event: an interschool English literature quiz. Each team to consist of two members. I'll come straight to the point. I have suggested to Miss Brockway that Zolile High and Camdeboo High join forces and enter a combined team. As I have already told you, she has agreed and so has the Festival director who I spoke to on the telephone this morning. There you have it Isabel Dyson. I anxiously await your response.

ISABEL: I'm in the team?

MR. M: Yes.

ISABEL: And. . . ? *(Her eyes brighten with anticipation)*

MR. M: That's right.

ISABEL: Thami!

MR. M: Correct!

ISABEL: Mr. M, you're a genius!

MR. M *(Holding up a hand to stop what was obviously going to be a very enthusiastic response)*: Wait! Wait! Before you get carried away and say yes, let me warn you about a few things. It's going to mean a lot of very hard work. I am appointing myself team coach and as Thami will tell you, I can be a very hard taskmaster. You'll have to give up a lot of free time young lady.

ISABEL: Anything else?

MR. M: Not for the moment.

ISABEL: Then I'll say it again. Mr. M, you're a genius! *(Her joy is enormous, and she shows it)* How's that for unruly behavior?

MR. M: The very worst! They couldn't do it better on the location streets. What a heartwarming response Isabel.

ISABEL: What were you expecting? That I would say no?

MR. M: I didn't know what to expect. I knew that you would give me a sympathetic hearing, but that I would be swept off my feet, literally and figuratively . . . no. I was most certainly not prepared for that. Does my silly little idea really mean that much to you?

ISABEL: None of that, Mr. M! It's not silly and it's not little and you know it.

MR. M: All right. But does it really mean that much to you?

ISABEL: Yes it does.

MR. M (*Persistent*): But why?

ISABEL: That visit to Zolile was one of the best things that has happened to me. I don't want it to just end there. One visit and that's it.

Mr. M listens quietly, attentively, an invitation to Isabel to say more.

It feels like it could be the beginning of something. I've met you and Thami and all the others and I would like to get to know you all better. But how do I do that? I can't just go after you chaps like . . . well, you know what I mean. Roll up and knock on your doors like you were neighbors or just living down the street. It's not as easy as that with us is it. You're in the location I'm in the town . . . and all the rest of it. So there I was feeling more and more frustrated about it all when along you come with your "silly little" idea. It's perfect! Do I make sense?

MR. M: Most definitely. Make some more.

ISABEL: I've been thinking about it you see. When I told my mom and dad about the debate and what a good time I'd had, I could see that they didn't really understand what I was talking about. Specially my mom. I ended up getting very impatient with her which wasn't very smart of me because the harder I tried to make her understand the more nervous she got. Anyway, I've cooled off now and I realize why she was like that. Being with black people on an equal footing, you know . . . as equals, because that is how I ended up feeling with Thami and his friends . . . that was something that had never happened to her. She didn't know what I was talking about. And because she knows nothing about it, she's frightened of it.

MR. M: You are not.

ISABEL: No. Not anymore.

MR. M: So you were.

ISABEL: Well, not so much frightened as sort of uncertain. You see, I thought I knew what to expect, but after a few minutes in Number One Classroom I realized I was wrong by a mile.

MR. M: What had you expected, Isabel?

ISABEL: You know, that everybody would be nice and polite and very, very grateful.

MR. M: And we weren't?

ISABEL: You were, but not them. Thami and his friends. *(She laughs at the memory) Ja*, to be honest Mr. M, that family of yours *was* a bit scary at first. But not anymore! I feel I've made friends with Thami . . . and the others, so now it's different.

MR. M: Simple as that.

ISABEL: Simple as that.

MR. M: Knowledge has banished fear.

ISABEL: That's right.

MR. M: Bravo. Bravo. And yet again Bravo! If you knew what it meant to me to hear you speak like that. I wasn't wrong. From the moment I first shook hands with you I knew you were a kindred spirit.

ISABEL: Tell me more about the competition.

MR. M: First prize is five thousand rand which the bank has stipulated must be spent on books for the school library. We will obviously divide it equally between Camdeboo and Zolile when you and Thami win.

ISABEL: Yes, what about my teammate. What does he say? Have you asked him yet?

MR. M: No, I haven't *asked* him Isabel, and I won't. I will *tell* him, and when I do I trust he will express as much enthusiasm for the idea as you have. I am an old-fashioned traditionalist in most things young lady, and my classroom is certainly no exception. I Teach, Thami Learns. He understands and accepts that that is the way it should be. You don't like the sound of that do you.

ISABEL: Does sound a bit dictatorial you know.

MR. M: It might sound that way but I assure you it isn't. We do not blur the difference between the generations in the way that you white people do. Respect for authority, right authority, is deeply ingrained in the African soul. It's all I've got when I stand there in Number One. Respect for my authority is my only teaching aid. If I ever lost it those young people will abandon their desks and take to the streets. I expect Thami to trust my judgment of what is best for him, and he does. That trust is the most sacred responsibility in my life.

ISABEL: He's your favorite, isn't he?

MR. M: Good Heavens! A good teacher doesn't have favorites! Are you suggesting that I might be a bad one? Because if you are . . . *(Looking around)* you would be right young lady. Measured by that yardstick I am a very bad teacher indeed. He *is* my favorite. Thami Mbikwana! Yes, I have waited a long time for him. To tell you the truth I had given up all hope of him ever coming along. Any teacher who takes his calling seriously dreams about that one special pupil, that one eager and gifted young head into

which he can pour all that he knows and loves and who
will justify all the years of frustration in the classroom.
There have been pupils that I'm proud of, but I've always
had to bully them into doing their schoolwork. Not with
Thami. *He* wants to learn the way other boys want to run
out of the classroom and make mischief. If he looks after
himself he'll go far and do big things. He's a born leader
Isabel, and that is what your generation needs. Powerful
forces are fighting for the souls of you young people. You
need *real* leaders. Not rabble-rousers. I know Thami is
meant to be one. I know it with such certainty it makes
me frightened. Because it is a responsibility. Mine and
mine alone.

I've got a small confession to make. In addition to
everything I've already said, there's another reason for this
idea of mine. When you and Thami shine at the Festival,
as I know you will, and win first prize and we've pocketed
a nice little check for five thousand rand, I am going to
point to Thami and say: And now ladies and gentlemen, a
full university scholarship if you please.

ISABEL: And you'll get it. We'll shine, we'll win, we'll pocket
that check and Thami will get a scholarship.

Mr. M's turn for an enthusiastic response.

MR. M *(Embarrassment and laughter)*: Your unruly behavior is
very infectious!

ISABEL: *My* unruly behavior? I like that! I caught that disease
in the location I'll have you know.

MR. M: The future is ours Isabel. We'll show this stupid
country how it is done.

ISABEL: When do we start?

MR. M: Next week. We need to plan our campaign very
carefully.

ISABEL: I'll be ready.

SCENE 4

Mr. M alone. He talks directly to the audience.

MR. M: "I am a man who in the eager pursuit of knowledge forgets his food and in the joy of its attainment forgets his sorrows, and who does not perceive that old age is coming on."

(He shakes his head) No. As I'm sure you have already guessed, that is not me. My pursuit of knowledge is eager, but I do perceive, and only too clearly, that old age is coming on, and at the best of times I do a bad job of forgetting my sorrows. Those wonderful words come from the finest teacher I have ever had, that most wise of all the ancient philosophers . . . Confucius! Yes. I am a Confucian. A black Confucian! There are not many of us. In fact I think there's a good chance that the only one in the country is talking to you at this moment.

I claim him as my teacher because I have read very carefully, and many times, and I will read it many times more, a little book I have about him, his life, his thoughts and utterances. Truly, they *are* wonderful words my friends, wonderful, wonderful words! My classroom motto comes from its pages: "Learning undigested by thought is labor lost. Thought unassisted by learning is perilous!" But the words that challenge me most these days, is something he said towards the end of his life. At the age of seventy he turned to his pupils one day and said that he could do whatever his heart prompted, without transgressing what was right.

What do you say to that?

Think about it. *Anything* his heart prompted, *anything* that rose up as a spontaneous urge in his soul, *without* transgressing what was right!

What a heart my friends! Aren't you envious of old
Confucius? Wouldn't it be marvelous to have a heart you
could trust like that? Imagine being able to wake up in
the morning in your little room, yawn and stretch, scratch
a few fleabites and then jump out of your bed and eat your
bowl of *mealie-pap* and sour milk with a happy heart
because you know that when you walk out into the world
you will be free to obey and act out, with a clear
conscience, all the promptings of your heart. No matter
what you see out there on the battle grounds of location
streets, and believe me, there are days now when my
eyesight feels more like a curse than a blessing, no matter
what stories of hardship and suffering you hear, or how
bad the news you read in the newspaper, knowing that the
whole truth, which can't be printed, is even worse . . . in
spite of all that, you need have no fear of your spontaneous
urges, because in obeying them you will not transgress
what is right.

(Another shake of his head, another rueful smile) No yet
again. Not in this life, and most certainly not in this
world where I find myself, will those wonderful words of
Confucius ever be mine. Not even if I lived to be one
hundred and seventy will I end up a calm, gentle Chinese
heart like his. I wish I could. Believe me, I really wish I
could. Because I am frightened of the one I've got. I don't
get gentle promptings from it my friends. I get heart
attacks. When I walk out into those streets, and I see
what is happening to my people, it jumps out and savages
me like a wild beast. *(Thumping his chest with a clenched fist)*
I've got a whole zoo in here, a mad zoo of hungry animals
. . . and the keeper is frightened! All of them. Mad and
savage!

Look at me! I'm sweating today. I've been sweating for
a week. Why? Because one of those animals, the one

called Hope, has broken loose and is looking for food.
Don't be fooled by its gentle name. It is as dangerous as
Hate and Despair would be if they ever managed to break
out. You think I'm exaggerating? Pushing my metaphor a
little too far? Then I'd like to put you inside a black skin
and ask you to keep Hope alive, find food for it on these
streets where our children, our loved and precious children
go hungry and die of malnutrition. No, believe me, it is a
dangerous animal for a black man to have prowling around
in his heart. So how do I manage to keep mine alive, you
ask. Friends, I am going to let you in on a terrible secret.
That is why I am a teacher.

It is all part of a secret plan to keep alive this savage
Hope of mine. The truth is that I am worse than Nero
feeding Christians to the lions. I feed young people to my
Hope. Every young body behind a school desk keeps it
alive.

So you've been warned! If you see a hungry gleam in
my eyes when I look at your children . . . you know what
it means. That is the monster that stands here before you.
Full name: Anela Myalatya. Age: fifty-seven. Marital
status: bachelor. Occupation: teacher. Address: the back
room of the Reverend Mbopa's house next to the Anglican
Church of St. Mark. It's a little on the small side. You
know those big kitchen-size boxes of matches they sell
these days . . . well if you imagine one of those as
Number One Classroom at Zolile High, then the little
matchbox you put in your pocket is my room at the
Reverend Mbopa's. But I'm not complaining. It has got all
I need . . . a table and chair where I correct homework
and prepare lessons, a comfortable bed for a good night's
insomnia and a reserved space for my chair in front of the
television set in the Reverend Mbopa's lounge.

So there you have it. What I call my life rattles around

in these two matchboxes . . . the classroom and the back
room. If you see me hurrying along the streets you can be
reasonably certain that one of those two is my urgent
destination. The people tease me. "Faster Mr. M" they
shout to me from their front doors. "You'll be late." They
think it's a funny joke. They don't know how close they
are to a terrible truth . . .

Yes! The clocks are ticking my friends. History has got
a strict timetable. If we're not careful we might be
remembered as the country where everybody arrived too
late.

SCENE 5

*Mr. M waiting. Isabel hurries on, carrying hockey stick and
togs, and her bookbag. She is hot and exhausted.*

ISABEL: Sorry Mr. M, sorry. The game started late.

MR. M: I haven't been waiting long.

Isabel unburdens herself and collapses with a groan.

Did you win?

ISABEL: No. We played a team of friendly Afrikaans-speaking
young Amazons from Jansenville and they licked us
hollow. Four-one! It was brutal! God they were fit. And
fast. They ran circles around us on that hockey field. I felt
so stupid. I kept saying to myself "It's only a game Isabel.
Relax! Enjoy it! Have a good time!" But no, there I was
swearing under my breath at poor little Hilary Castle for
being slow and not getting into position for my passes.

(Laughing at herself) You want to know something really
terrible? A couple of times I actually wanted to go over
and hit her with my hockey stick. Isn't that awful? It's no
good Mr. M, I've got to face it: I'm a bad loser. Got any
advice for me?

MR. M: On how to be a good one?

ISABEL: *Ja.* How to lose graciously. With dignity. I mean it. I really wish I could.

MR. M: If I did have advice for you Isabel, I think I would be well advised to try it out on myself first . . .

ISABEL: Why? You one as well?

Mr. M nods.

I don't believe it.

MR. M: It's true, Isabel. I'm ashamed to say it but when I lose I also want to grab my hockey stick and hit somebody.

A good laugh from Isabel.

Believe me I can get very petty and mean if I'm not on the winning side. I suppose most bachelors end up like that. We get so used to having everything our own way that when something goes wrong . . . !

So there's my advice to you. Get married! If what I've heard is true, holy matrimony is the best school of all for learning how to lose.

ISABEL: I don't think it's something you can learn. You've either got it or you haven't. Like Thami. Without even thinking about it I know *he's* a good loser.

MR. M: Maybe.

ISABEL: No. No maybes about it. He'd never grab his hockey stick and take it out on somebody else if he didn't win.

MR. M: You're right. I can't see him doing that. You've become good friends, haven't you?

ISABEL: The best. These past few weeks have been quite an education. I owe you a lot you know. I think Thami would say the same . . . if you would only give him the chance to do so.

MR. M: What do you mean by that remark, young lady?

ISABEL: You know what I mean by that remark, *Mr. Teacher!* It's called Freedom of Speech.

MR. M: I've given him plenty of Freedom, within reasonable limits, but he never uses it.

ISABEL: Because you're *always* the teacher and he's *always* the pupil. Stop teaching him all the time Mr. M. Try just talking to him for a change . . . you know, like a friend. I bet you in some ways I already know more about Thami than you.

MR. M: I don't deny that. In which case tell me, is he happy?

ISABEL: What do you mean? Happy with what? Us? The competition?

MR. M: Yes, and also his schoolwork and . . . everything else.

ISABEL: Why don't you ask him?

MR. M: Because all I'll get is another polite "Yes Teacher." I thought maybe he had said something to you about the way he really felt.

ISABEL *(Shaking her head)*: The two of you! It's crazy!

But *ja*, he's happy. At least I think he is. He's not a blabbermouth like me, Mr. M. He doesn't give much away . . . even when we talk about ourselves. I don't know what it was like in your time, but being eighteen years old today is a pretty complicated business as far as we're concerned. If you asked me if I was happy, I'd say yes, but that doesn't mean I haven't got any problems. I've got plenty and I'm sure it's the same with Thami.

MR. M: Thami has told you he's got problems?

ISABEL: Come on, Mr. M! We've all got problems. I've got problems, you've got problems, Thami's got problems.

MR. M: But did he say what they were?

ISABEL: You're fishing for something, Mr. M. What is it?

MR. M: Trouble, Isabel. I'm sorry to say it, but I'm fishing for Trouble and I'm trying to catch it before it gets too big.

ISABEL: Thami is in trouble?

MR. M: Not yet, but he will be if he's not careful. And all his friends as well. It's swimming around everywhere trying to stir up things. In the classroom, out on the streets.

ISABEL: Oh, you mean that sort of trouble. Is it really as bad as people are saying?

MR. M: There's a dangerous, reckless mood in the location. Specially among the young people. Very silly things are being said Isabel, and I've got a suspicion that even sillier things are being whispered among themselves. I know Thami trusts you. I was wondering if he had told you what they were whispering about.

ISABEL *(Shocked by what Mr. M is asking of her)*: Wow! That's a hard one you're asking for Mr. M. Just suppose he had, do you think it would be right for me to tell you? *We* call that splitting, you know, and you're not very popular if you're caught doing it.

MR. M: It would be for his own good Isabel.

ISABEL: Well he hasn't . . . thank God! So I don't have to deal with that one. *(Pause)* If I ever did that to him, and he found out, that would be the end of our friendship you know. I wish you hadn't asked me.

MR. M *(Realizing his mistake)*: Forgive me Isabel. I'm just over-anxious on his behalf. One silly mistake now could ruin everything. Forget that I asked you and . . . please . . . don't mention anything about our little chat to Thami. I'll find time to have a word with him myself.

Thami appears, also direct from the sports field.

THAMI: Hi folks. Sorry I'm late.

ISABEL: I've just got here myself. Mr. M is the one who's been waiting.

THAMI: Sorry teacher. The game went into extra time.

ISABEL: Did you win?

THAMI: No. We lost one-nil.

ISABEL: Good.

THAMI: But it was a good game. We're trying out some new combinations and they nearly worked. The chaps are really

starting to come together as a team. A little more
practice, that's all we need.

ISABEL: Hear that, Mr. M? What did I tell you. And look at
him. Smiling! Happy! Even in defeat, a generous word for
his teammates.

THAMI: What's going on?

ISABEL: Don't try to look innocent Mbikwana. Your secret is
out. Your true identity has been revealed. You are a good
loser, and don't try to deny it.

THAMI: Me? You're wrong. I don't like losing.

ISABEL: It's not a question of liking or not liking, but of
being able to do so without a crooked smile on your face,
a knot in your stomach and murder in your heart.

THAMI: You lost your game this afternoon.

ISABEL: Whatever made you guess! We were trounced. So be
careful. I'm looking for revenge.

MR. M: Good! Then let's see if you can get it in the arena of
English literature. What do we deal with today?

THAMI: Nineteenth-century poetry.

MR. M *(With relish)*: Beautiful! Beautiful! Beautiful! *(Making
himself comfortable)* Whose service?

*Thami picks up a stone, hands behind his back, then clenched
fists for Isabel to guess. She does. She wins. Their relationship is
now obviously very relaxed and easy.*

ISABEL: Gird your loins, Mbikwana. I want blood.

THAMI: I wish you the very best of luck.

ISABEL: God, I hate you.

MR. M: First service, please.

ISABEL: Right. I'll give you an easy one to start with. The
Lake Poets. Name them.

THAMI: Wordsworth . . .

ISABEL: Yes, he was one. Who else?

THAMI: Wordsworth and . . .

ISABEL: There was only one Wordsworth.

THAMI: I pass.

ISABEL: Wordsworth, Southey and Coleridge.

THAMI: I should have guessed Coleridge!

MR. M: One-love.

ISABEL: First line of a poem by each of them please.

THAMI: Query Mr. Umpire . . . how many questions is that?

MR. M: One at a time please Isabel.

ISABEL: Coleridge.

THAMI: "In Xanadu did Kubla Khan
A stately pleasure dome decree . . ."
And if you don't like that one what about:
" 'Tis the middle of the night by the castle clock,
And the owls have awakened the crowing cock;
Tu—whit! Tu—whoo!"
And if you're still not satisfied . . .

ISABEL: Stop showing off young man.

MR. M: One-all.

ISABEL: Wordsworth.

THAMI: "Earth has not anything to show more fair:
Dull would he be of soul who could pass by
A sight so touching in its majesty . . ."

MR. M: One-two.

ISABEL: Southey.

THAMI: Pass.

ISABEL: "From his brimstone bed at break of day
A-walking the Devil is gone . . .
His jacket was red and his breeches were blue,
And there was a hole where the tail came through."

THAMI: Hey, I like that one!

ISABEL: A poet laureate to boot.

MR. M: Two-all.

ISABEL: One of them was expelled from school. Who was it
and why?

THAMI: Wordsworth. For smoking in the lavatory.

ISABEL *(After a good laugh)*: You're terrible Thami. He should be penalized Mr. Umpire . . . for irreverence! It was Southey and the reason he was expelled—you're going to like this—was for writing a "precocious" essay against flogging.

THAMI: How about that!

MR. M: Three-two. Change service.

THAMI: I am not going to show you any mercy. What poet was born with deformed feet, accused of incest and died of fever while helping the Greeks fight for freedom? "A love of liberty characterizes his poems and the desire to see the fettered nations of Europe set free."

ISABEL: Byron.

THAMI: Lord Byron if you please.

MR. M: Two-four.

ISABEL: One of your favorites.

THAMI: You bet.

"Yet, Freedom! yet thy banner, torn, but flying,
Streams like the thunder-storm *against* the wind."

Do you know the Christian names of Lord Byron?

ISABEL: Oh dammit! . . . it's on the tip of my tongue. Henry?

Thami shakes his head.

Herbert?

THAMI: How many guesses does she get, Mr. Umpire?

ISABEL: All right, give him the point. I pass.

THAMI: George Gordon.

MR. M: Three-four.

THAMI: To whom was he unhappily married for one long year?

ISABEL: Pass.

THAMI: Anne Isabella Milbanke.

MR. M: Four-all.

THAMI: Father's occupation?

ISABEL: Pass.

THAMI: John Byron was a captain in the army.

MR. M: Five-four.

THAMI: What other great poet was so overcome with grief when he heard news of Lord Byron's death, that he went out and carved into a rock: "Byron is dead."

ISABEL: Matthew Arnold?

THAMI: No. Another aristocrat . . . Alfred Lord Tennyson.

MR. M: Six-four. Change service.

ISABEL: Right. Whose body did your Lord Byron burn on a beach in Italy?

THAMI: Shelley.

MR. M: Four-seven.

ISABEL: And what happened to Mr. Shelley's ashes?

THAMI: In a grave beside John Keats in Rome.

MR. M: Four-eight.

ISABEL: Shelley's wife. What is she famous for?

THAMI: Which one? There were two. Harriet Westbrook, sixteen years old, who he abandoned after three years and who drowned herself? Or number two wife—who I think is the one you're interested in—Mary Wollstonecraft, the author of *Frankenstein*.

MR. M: Four-nine.

ISABEL: How much?

MR. M: Four-nine.

ISABEL: I don't believe this! *(She grabs her hockey stick)*

THAMI *(Enjoying himself immensely)*: I crammed in two poets last night, Isabel. Guess who they were?

ISABEL: Byron and Shelley. In that case we will deal with Mr. John Keats. What profession did he abandon in order to devote himself to poetry?

THAMI: Law.

ISABEL: You're guessing and you're wrong. He qualified as a surgeon.

MR. M: Five-nine.

ISABEL: What epitaph, composed by himself, is engraved on his tombstone in Rome?

THAMI: Pass.

ISABEL: "Here lies one whose name was writ on water."

MR. M: Six-nine. Let's leave the Births, Marriages and Deaths column please. I want to hear some more poetry.

THAMI: Whose service?

MR. M: Yours.

THAMI: "I must go down to the seas again, to the lonely sea and the sky,

And all I ask is a tall ship and a star to steer her by . . ."

ISABEL: "And the wheel's kick and the wind's song and the white sail's shaking,

And a grey mist on the sea's face and a grey dawn breaking. . . .

I must go down to the seas again to the vagrant gypsy life,

To the gull's way and the whale's way where the wind's like a whetted knife . . ."

THAMI: "And all I ask is a merry yarn from a laughing fellow-rover,

And quiet sleep and a sweet dream when the long trick's over."

MR. M: Bravo! Bravo! Bravo! But who gets the point?

ISABEL: Give it to John Masefield, Mr. Umpire. *(To Thami)* Nineteenth century?

THAMI: He was born in 1878. To tell you the truth I couldn't resist it. You choose one.

ISABEL: "I met a traveller from an antique land

Who said: Two vast and trunkless legs of stone

Stand in the desert . . . Near them, on the sand,
Half sunk, a shattered visage lies, whose frown,
And wrinkled lip, and sneer of cold command,
Tell that its sculptor well those passions read
Which yet survive, stamped on these lifeless things,
The hand that mocked them, and the heart that fed:
And on the pedestal these words appear:"

THAMI: "My name is Ozymandias, king of kings:
Look on my works, ye Mighty, and despair!"

ISABEL: "Nothing beside remains. Round the decay
Of that colossal wreck, boundless and bare
The lone and level sands stretch far away."

THAMI: And that point goes to Mr. Shelley.

ISABEL (*Takes notebook from her bookbag*): You'll be interested to know gentlemen that Ozymandias is not a fiction of Mr. Shelley's very fertile imagination. He was a real, live Egyptian king. Rameses the Second! According to *Everyman's Encyclopedia* . . . "One of the most famous of the Egyptian kings . . . erected many monuments . . . but his oppressive rule left Egypt impoverished and suffering from an incurable decline."

THAMI: What happened to the statue?

ISABEL: You mean how was it toppled?

THAMI: Yes.

ISABEL: Didn't say. Weather I suppose. And time. Two thousand four hundred B.C. . . . That's over four thousand years ago. Why? What were you thinking?

THAMI: I had a book of Bible stories when I was small, and there was a picture in it showing the building of the pyramids by the slaves. Thousands of them, like ants, pulling the big blocks of stone with ropes, being guarded by soldiers with whips and spears. According to that picture the slaves must have easily outnumbered the soldiers one hundred to one. I actually tried to count them all one day but the drawing wasn't good enough for that.

ISABEL: What are you up to, Mbikwana? Trying to stir up a little social unrest in the time of the Pharaohs, are you?

THAMI: Don't joke about it Miss Dyson. There are quite a few Ozymandiases in this country waiting to be toppled. And you'll see it happen. *We* won't leave it to Time to bring them down.

Mr. M has been listening to the exchange between Thami and Isabel very attentively.

MR. M *(Trying to put a smile on it)*: Who is the *we* you speak of with such authority Thami?

THAMI: The People.

MR. M *(Recognition)*: Yes, yes, yes, of course . . . I should have known. "The People" . . . with a capital P. Does that include me? Am I one of "The People"?

THAMI: If you choose to be.

MR. M: I've got to choose have I. My black skin doesn't confer automatic membership. So how do I go about choosing?

THAMI: By identifying with the fight for our Freedom.

MR. M: As simple as that? Then I am most definitely one of "The People." I want our Freedom as much as any of you. In fact, I was fighting for it in my own small way long before you were born! But I've got a small problem. Does that noble fight of ours really have to stoop to pulling down a few silly statues? Where do you get the idea that we, "The People," want you to do that for us?

THAMI *(Trying)*: They are not our heroes, teacher.

MR. M: They are not our statues Thami! Wouldn't it be better for us to rather put our energies into erecting a few of our own? We've also got heroes, you know.

THAMI: Like who, Mr. M? Nelson Mandela? *(Shaking his head with disbelief)* Hey! *They* would pull *that* statue down so fast—

MR. M *(Cutting him off)*: In which case they would be just as guilty of gross vandalism . . . because that is what it will be, regardless of who does it to whom. Destroying somebody else's property is inexcusable behavior!

No Thami. As one of the People you claim to be acting for, I raise my hand in protest. Please don't pull down any statues on my behalf. Don't use me as an excuse for an act of Lawlessness. If you want to do something "revolutionary" for me let us sit down and discuss it, because I have a few constructive alternatives I would like to suggest. Do I make myself clear?

THAMI: Yes teacher.

MR. M: Good. I'm glad we understand each other.

ISABEL *(Intervening)*: So, what's next? Mr. M? How about singling out a few specific authors who we know will definitely come up. Like Dickens. I bet you anything you like there'll be questions about him and his work.

MR. M: Good idea. We'll concentrate on novelists. A short list of hot favorites.

ISABEL: Thomas Hardy . . . Jane Austen . . . who else, Thami?

MR. M: Put your heads together and make a list. I want twenty names. Divide it between the two of you and get to work. I must be on my way.

ISABEL: Just before you go Mr. M, I've got an invitation for you and Thami from my mom and dad. Would the two of you like to come to tea one afternoon?

MR. M: What a lovely idea!

ISABEL: They've had enough of me going on and on about the all-knowing Mr. M and his brilliant protégé Thami. They want to meet you for themselves. Thami? All right with you?

MR. M: Of course we accept Isabel. It will be a pleasure and a privilege for us to meet Mr. and Mrs. Dyson. Tell them we accept most gratefully.

ISABEL: Next Sunday.

MR. M: Perfect.

ISABEL: Thami?

MR. M: Don't worry about him, Isabel. I'll put it in my diary
and remind him at school.

Mr. M leaves.

ISABEL *(Sensitive to a change of mood in Thami)*: I think you'll
like my folks. My mom's a bit on the reserved side but
that's just because she's basically very shy. But you and my
dad should get on well. Start talking sport with him and
he won't let you go. He played cricket for E.P. you know.
(Pause) You will come, won't you?

THAMI *(Edge to his voice)*: Didn't you hear Mr. M? "A delight
and a privilege! We accept most gratefully." *(Writing in his
notebook)* Charles Dickens . . . Thomas Hardy . . . Jane
Austen . . .

ISABEL: Was he speaking for you as well?

THAMI: He speaks for me on nothing!

ISABEL: Relax . . . I know that. That's why I tried to ask you
separately and why I'll ask you again. Would you like to
come to tea next Sunday to meet my family? It's not a
polite invitation. They really want to meet you.

THAMI: Me? Why? Are they starting to get nervous?

ISABEL: Oh come off it Thami. Don't be like that. They're
always nervous when it comes to me. But this time it
happens to be genuine interest. I've told you. I talk about
you at home. They know I have a good time with you
. . . that we're a team . . . which they are now very
proud of incidentally . . . and that we're cramming like
lunatics so that we can put up a good show at the
Festival. Is it so strange that they want to meet you after
all that? Honestly, sometimes dealing with the two of you
is like walking on a tightrope. I'm always scared I'm

going to put a foot wrong and . . . well I just *hate* being
scared like that.

A few seconds of truculent silence between the two of them.

What's going on Thami? Between you two? There's
something very wrong isn't there?

THAMI: No more than usual.

ISABEL: No you don't. A hell of a lot more than usual and
don't deny it because it's getting to be pretty obvious. I
mean I know he gets on your nerves. I knew that the first
day we met. But it's more than that now. These past
couple of meetings I've caught you looking at him,
watching him in a . . . I don't know . . . in a sort of
hard way. Very critical. Not just once. Many times. Do
you know you're doing it?

Shrug of the shoulders from Thami.

Well if you know it or not you are. And now he's started
as well.

THAMI: What do you mean?

ISABEL: He's watching you.

THAMI: So? He can watch me as much as he likes. I've got
nothing to hide. Even if I had he'd be the last person to
find out. He sees nothing Isabel.

ISABEL: I think you are very wrong.

THAMI: No, I'm not. That's his trouble. He's got eyes and ears
but he sees nothing and hears nothing.

ISABEL: Go on. Please. *(Pause)* I mean it Thami. I want to
know what's going on.

THAMI: He is out of touch with what is really happening to us
blacks and the way we feel about things. He thinks the
world is still the way it was when he was young. It's not!
It's different now, but he's too blind to see it. He doesn't
open his eyes and ears and see what is happening around
him or listen to what people are saying.

ISABEL: What are they saying?

THAMI: They've got no patience left, Isabel. They want change. They want it now!

ISABEL: But he agrees with that. He never stops saying it himself.

THAMI: No. His ideas about change are the old-fashioned ones. And what have they achieved? Nothing. We are worse off now than we ever were. The people don't want to listen to his kind of talk anymore.

ISABEL: I'm still lost, Thami. What kind of talk is that?

THAMI: You've just heard it, Isabel. It calls our struggle vandalism and lawless behavior. It's the sort of talk that expects us to do nothing and wait quietly for white South Africa to wake up. If we listen to it our grandchildren still won't know what it means to be Free.

ISABEL: And those old-fashioned ideas of his . . . are we one of them?

THAMI: What do you mean?

ISABEL: You and me. The competition.

THAMI: Let's change the subject, Isabel. *(From his notebook)* Charles Dickens . . . Thomas Hardy . . . Jane Austen . . .

ISABEL: No! You can't do that! I'm involved. I've got a right to know. Are we an old-fashioned idea?

THAMI: Not our friendship. That is our decision, our choice.

ISABEL: And the competition?

THAMI *(Uncertain of himself)*: Maybe . . . I'm not sure. I need time to think about it.

ISABEL *(Foreboding)*: Oh boy. This doesn't sound so good. You've got to talk to him Thami.

THAMI: He won't listen.

ISABEL: Make him listen!

THAMI: It doesn't work that way with us Isabel. You can't just stand up and tell your teacher he's got the wrong ideas.

ISABEL: Well that's just your bad luck because you are going to have to do it. Even if it means breaking sacred rules and traditions, you have got to stand up and have it out with him.

I don't think you realize what all of this means to him. It's a hell of a lot more than just an "old-fashioned idea" as far as he's concerned. This competition, you and me, but especially you, Thami Mbikwana, has become a sort of crowning achievement to his life as a teacher. It's become a sort of symbol for him, and if it were to all suddenly collapse. . . ! No. I don't want to think about it.

THAMI *(Flash of anger and impatience)*: Then don't! Please leave it alone now and just let's get on with whatever it is we've got to do.

ISABEL: Right, if that's the way you want it . . . *(From her notebook)* Charles Dickens, Thomas Hardy, Jane Austen . . . who else?

THAMI: I'm sorry. I know you're only trying to help but you've got to understand that it's not just a personal issue between him and me. That would be easy. I don't think I would care then. Just wait for the end of the year and then get out of that classroom and that school as fast as I can. But there is more to it than that. I've told you before: sitting in a classroom doesn't mean the same thing to me that it does to you. That classroom is a political reality in my life—it's a part of the whole political system we're up against and Mr. M has chosen to identify himself with it.

ISABEL *(Trying a new tack)*: All right. I believe you. I accept everything you said . . . about him, your relationship, the situation . . . no arguments. Okay? But doesn't all of that only make it still more important that the two of you start talking to each other? I know *he* wants to, but he doesn't know how to start. It's *so* sad . . . because I can see him trying to reach out to you. Show him how it's done. Make the first move. Oh Thami, don't let it go wrong between the two of you. That's just about the worst thing I could imagine. We all need each other.

THAMI: I don't need him.

ISABEL: I think you do, just as much as he—

THAMI: Don't tell me what I need, Isabel! And stop telling me what to do! You don't know what my life is about, so keep your advice to yourself.

ISABEL: I'm sorry. I don't mean to interfere. I thought we were a team and that what involved you two concerned me as well. I'll mind my own business in future. *(She is deeply hurt. She collects her things)* Let's leave it at that then. See you next week . . . I hope!

(Starts to leave, stops, returns and confronts him) You used the word *friendship* a few minutes ago. It's a beautiful word and I'll do anything to make it true for us. But don't let's cheat Thami. If we can't be open and honest with each other and say what is in our hearts, we've got no right to use it. *(She leaves)*

SCENE 6

Thami alone.

THAMI *(Singing)*:
Masiye Masiye Skolweni
Masiye Masiye Skolweni
Eskolweni Sasakhaya
Eskolweni Sasakhaya (Repeat)

Gongo Gongo
Iyakhala Intsimbi
Gongo Gongo
Iyakhala Intsimbi

(Translating)

Come, come, let's go to school
Let's go to our very own school

Gongo Gongo
The bell is ringing
Gongo Gongo
The bell is calling!

Singing that at the top of his voice and holding his slate under his arm, seven-year-old Thami Mbikwana marched proudly with the other children every morning into his classroom.

Gongo Gongo
The school bell is ringing!

And what a wonderful sound that was for me. Starting with the little farm school, I remember my school bells like beautiful voices calling to me all through my childhood . . . and I came running when they did. You should have seen me man. In junior school I was the first one at the gates every morning. I was waiting there when the caretaker came to unlock them. Oh yes! Young Thami was a very eager scholar. And what made it even better, he was also one of the clever ones. "A most particularly promising pupil" is how one of my school reports described me. My first real scholastic achievement was a composition I wrote about myself in Standard Two. Not only did it get me top marks in the class, the teacher was so proud of me, she made me read it out to the whole school at assembly.

(His composition) "The story of my life so far. By Thami

Mbikwana. The story of my life so far is not yet finished because I am only ten years old and I am going to live a long long time. I come from Kingwilliamstown. My father is Amos Mbikwana and he works very hard for the *baas* on the railway. I am also going to work very hard and get good marks in all my classes and make my teacher very happy. The story of my life so far has also got a very happy ending because when I am big I am going to be a doctor so that I can help my people. I will drive to the hospital every day in a big, white ambulance full of nurses. I will make black people better free of charge. The white people must pay me for my medicine because they have got lots of money. That way I will also get lots of money. My mother and my father will stop working and come and live with me in a big house. That is the story of my life up to where I am in Standard Two."

I must bring my story up to date because there have been some changes and developments since little Thami wrote those hopeful words eight years ago. To start with I don't think I want to be a doctor anymore. That praiseworthy ambition has unfortunately died in me. It still upsets me very much when I think about the pain and suffering of my people, but I realize now that what causes most of it is not an illness that can be cured by the pills and bottles of medicine they hand out at the clinic. I don't need to go to university to learn what my people really need is a strong double-dose of that traditional old Xhosa remedy called *"Inkululeke."* Freedom. So right now I'm not sure what I want to be anymore. It's hard, you see, for us "bright young blacks" to dream about wonderful careers as doctors, or lawyers, when we keep waking up in a world which doesn't allow the majority of our people any dreams at all. But to get back to my composition, I did try my best to keep that promise I made in it. For a long time—Standard Three, Standard Four, Standard Five—I did work very hard and I did get good marks in all my subjects. This "most particularly promising pupil" made a lot of teachers very happy.

I'm sorry to say but I can't do it anymore. I have tried very hard, believe me, but it is not as simple and easy as it used to be to sit behind that desk and listen to the Teacher. That little world of the classroom where I used to be happy, where they used to pat me on the head and say: "Little Thami, you'll go far!"—that little room of wonderful promises, where I used to feel so safe, has become a place I don't trust anymore. Now I sit at my desk like an animal that has smelt danger, heard something moving in the bushes and knows it must be very, very careful.

At the beginning of this year the Inspector of Bantu Schools in the Cape Midlands Region, Mr. Dawid Grobbelaar—he makes us call him Oom Dawie—came to give us Standard Tens his usual pep talk. He does it every year. We know Oom Dawie well. He's been coming to Zolile for a long time. When he walked into our classroom we all jumped up as usual but he didn't want any of that. "Sit, sit. I'm not a bloody sergeant major." Oom Dawie believes he knows how to talk to us. He loosened his tie, took off his jacket and rolled up his sleeves. It was a very hot day.

"Dis better. *Nou kan ons lekker gesels.* Boys and girls or maybe I should say 'young men' and 'young women' now, because you are coming to the end of your time behind those desks . . . you are special! You are the elite! We have educated you because we want you to be major shareholders in the future of this wonderful Republic of ours. In fact, we want *all* the peoples of South Africa to share in that future . . . black, white, brown, yellow, and

if there are some green ones out there, then them as well."
Ho! Ho! Ho!

I don't remember much about what he said after that
because my head was trying to deal with that one word:
the Future! He kept using it . . . "our future," "the
country's future," "a wonderful future of peace and
prosperity." What does he really mean, I kept asking
myself. Why does my heart go hard and tight as a stone
when he says it? I look around me in the location at the
men and women who went out into that "wonderful
future" before me. What do I see? Happy and contented
shareholders in this exciting enterprise called the Republic
of South Africa? No. I see a generation of tired, defeated
men and women crawling back to their miserable little
pondoks at the end of a day's work for the white *baas* or
madam. And those are the lucky ones. They've at least got
work. Most of them are just sitting around wasting away
their lives while they wait helplessly for a miracle to feed
their families, a miracle that never comes.

Those men and women are our fathers and mothers. We
have grown up watching their humiliation. We have to
live every day with the sight of them begging for food in
this land of their birth, and their parents' birth . . . all
the way back to the first proud ancestors of our people.
Black people lived on this land for centuries before any
white settler had landed! Does Oom Dawie think we are
blind? That when we walk through the streets of the
white town we do not see the big houses and the beautiful
gardens with their swimming pools full of laughing
people, and compare it with what we've got, what we have
to call home? Or does Oom Dawie just think we are very
stupid? That in spite of the wonderful education he has
given us, we can't use the simple arithmetic of add and
subtract, multiply and divide to work out the rightful

share of twenty-five million black people?

Do you understand me, good people? Do you
understand now why it is not as easy as it used to be to
sit behind that desk and learn only what Oom Dawie has
decided I must know? My head is rebellious. It refuses
now to remember when the Dutch landed, and the
Huguenots landed, and the British landed. It has already
forgotten when the Old Union became the proud young
Republic. But it does know what happened in Kliptown
in 1955, in Sharpeville on twenty-first March 1960 and in
Soweto on the sixteenth of June 1976. Do you? Better find
out because those are dates your children will have to learn
one day. We don't need Zolile classrooms anymore. We
know now what they really are—traps which have been
carefully set to catch our minds, our souls. No, good
people. We have woken up at last. We have found another
school—the streets, the little rooms, the funeral parlors of
the location—anywhere the people meet and whisper
names we have been told to forget, the dates of events
they try to tell us never happened, and the speeches they
try to say were never made.

Those are the lessons we are eager and proud to learn,
because they are lessons about *our* history, about *our*
heroes. But the time for whispering them is past.
Tomorrow we start shouting.

AMANDLA!

ACT TWO

◆

SCENE 1

Isabel and Thami. Isabel has books and papers. From behind a relaxed and easy manner, she watches Thami carefully.

ISABEL: What I've done is write out a sort of condensed biography of all of them . . . you know, the usual stuff . . . date of birth, where they were born, where they died, who they married . . . et cetera, et cetera. My dad made copies for you and Mr. M. Sit. *(Hands over a set of papers to Thami)* You okay?

THAMI: *Ja, ja.*

ISABEL: For example . . . *(Reading)* Bronte sisters . . . I lumped them all together . . . Charlotte 1816–1855; Emily 1818–1848; Anne 1820–1849. . . . Can you

51

believe that? Not one of them reached the age of forty. Anne died when she was twenty-nine, Emily when she was thirty, and Charlotte reached the ripe old age of thirty-nine! Family home: Haworth, Yorkshire. First publication a joint volume of verse . . . *Poems by Currer, Ellis and Acton Bell*. All novels published under these nom de plumes. Charlotte the most prolific . . . *(Abandoning the notes)* Why am I doing this? You're not listening to me.

THAMI: Sorry.

ISABEL *(She waits for more, but that is all she gets)*: So? Should I carry on wasting my breath or do you want to say something?

THAMI: No, I must talk.

ISABEL: Good. I'm ready to listen.

THAMI: I don't know where to begin.

ISABEL: The deep end. Take my advice, go to the deep end and just jump right in. That's how I learnt to swim.

THAMI: No. I want to speak carefully because I don't want you to get the wrong ideas about what's happening and what I'm going to say. It's not like it's your fault, that it's because of anything you said or did . . . you know what I mean?

ISABEL: You don't want me to take personally whatever it is you are finding so hard to tell me.

THAMI: That's right. It's not about you and me personally. I've had a good time with you Isabel.

ISABEL: And I've had an important one with you.

THAMI: If it was just you and me, there wouldn't be a problem.

ISABEL: We've got a problem have we?

THAMI: I have.

ISABEL *(Losing patience)*: Oh for God's sake Thami. Stop trying to spare my feelings and just say it. If you are trying to tell me that I've been wasting my breath for a lot longer

than just this afternoon . . . just go ahead and say it! I'm
not a child. I can take it. Because that is what you are
trying to tell me isn't it? That it's all off.

THAMI: Yes.

ISABEL: The great literary quiz team is no more. You are
pulling out of the competition.

THAMI: Yes.

ISABEL: You shouldn't have made it so hard for yourself
Thami. It doesn't come as all that big a surprise. I've had
a feeling that something was going to go wrong
somewhere.

Been a strange time these past few weeks hasn't it?
At home, at school, in the shop . . . everywhere! Things
I've been seeing and doing my whole life, just don't feel
right anymore. Like my Saturday chats with Samuel — I
told you about him remember, he delivers for my dad —
well you should have heard the last one. It was
excruciating. It felt so false, and forced, and when I
listened to what I was saying and how I was saying it . . .
oh my God! Sounded as if I thought I was talking to a
ten-year-old. Halfway through our misery my dad barged
in and told me not to waste Samuel's time because he had
work to do which of course led to a flaming row between
me and my dad. . . . Am I changing Thami? My dad says
I am.

THAMI: In what way?

ISABEL: Forget it. The only thing I *do* know at this moment is
that I don't very much like the way anything feels right
now, starting with myself. So have you told Mr. M yet?

THAMI: No.

ISABEL: Good luck. I don't envy you that little conversation.
If I'm finding the news a bit hard to digest, I don't know
what he is going to do with it. I've just got to accept it. I
doubt very much if he will.

THAMI: He's got no choice Isabel. I've decided and that's the end of it.

ISABEL: So do you think we can at least talk about it? Help me to understand? Because to be absolutely honest with you Thami I don't think I do. You're not the only one with a problem. What Mr. M had to say about the team and the whole idea made a hell of a lot of sense to me. You owe it to me Thami. A lot more than just my spare time is involved.

THAMI: Talk about what? Don't you know what is going on?

ISABEL: Don't be stupid Thami! Of course I do! You'd have to be pretty dumb not to know that the dreaded "unrest" has finally reached us as well.

THAMI: We don't call it that. Our word for it is *"Isiqalo"* . . . The Beginning.

ISABEL: All right then, "The Beginning." I don't care what it's called. All I'm asking you to do is explain to me how the two of us learning some poetry, cramming in potted bios . . . interferes with all of that.

THAMI: Please just calm down and listen to me! I know you're angry and I don't blame you. I would be as well. But you must understand that pulling out of this competition is just a small side issue. There was a meeting in the location last night. It was decided to call for a general stay-at-home. We start boycotting classes tomorrow as part of that campaign.

ISABEL: Does Mr. M know about all of this?

THAMI: I think he does now.

ISABEL: Wasn't he at that meeting?

THAMI: The meeting was organized by the Comrades. He wasn't welcome.

ISABEL: Because his ideas are old-fashioned.

THAMI: Yes.

ISABEL: School boycott! Comrades! So our safe, contented little
Camdeboo is really going to find out what it's all about.
How long do you think it will last?

THAMI: I don't know. It's hard to say.

ISABEL: A week.

THAMI: No. It will be longer.

ISABEL: A month? Two months?

THAMI: We'll go back to school when the authorities scrap
Bantu Education and recognize and negotiate with Student
Committees. That was the resolution last night.

ISABEL: But when the boycott and . . . you know . . .
everything is all over could we carry on then, if there was
still time?

THAMI: I haven't thought about that.

ISABEL: So think about it. Please.

THAMI (*Nervous about a commitment*): It's hard to say Isabel . . .
but *ja* . . . maybe we could . . . I'm not sure.

ISABEL: Not much enthusiasm there, Mr. Mbikwana! You're
right. Why worry about a stupid competition. It will
most probably be too late anyway. So that's it then. Let's
just say we gave ourselves a crash course in English
literature.

Could have done a lot worse with our spare time,
couldn't we? I enjoyed myself. I read a lot of beautiful
poetry I might never have got around to. (*Uncertain of
herself*) It doesn't mean the end of everything though does
it? I mean, we can go on meeting, just as friends?

THAMI (*Warily*): When?

ISABEL: Oh . . . I mean, you know, like anytime. Next week!
(*Pause*) I'm not talking about the competition Thami. I
accept that it's dead. I think it's a pity . . . but so what.
I'm talking now about you and me just as friends.
(*She waits. She realizes. She collects herself*) So our

friendship *is* an old-fashioned idea after all. Well don't
waste your time here. You better get going and look after
. . . whatever it is that's beginning. And good luck!

Thami starts to go.

No! Thami come back here!! *(Struggling ineffectually to
control her anger and pain)* There is something very stupid
somewhere and it's most probably me but I can't help it
. . . *it just doesn't make sense!* I know it does to you and
I'm sure it's just my white selfishness and ignorance that is
stopping me from understanding *but it still doesn't make
sense.* Why can't we go on seeing each other and meeting
as friends? Tell me what is wrong with our friendship?

THAMI: You're putting words in my mouth Isabel. I didn't say
there was anything wrong with it. But others won't see it
the way we do.

ISABEL: Who? Your Comrades?

THAMI: Yes.

ISABEL: And they are going to decide whether we can or can't
be friends!

THAMI: I was right. You don't understand what's going on.

ISABEL: And you're certainly not helping me to.

THAMI *(Trying)*: Visiting you like this is dangerous. People
talk. U'sispumla . . . your maid . . . has seen me. She
could mention, just innocently but to the wrong person,
that Thami Mbikwana is visiting and having tea with the
white people she works for.

ISABEL: And of course that is such a big crime!

THAMI: In the eyes of the location . . . yes! My world is also
changing Isabel. I'm breaking the boycott by being here.
The Comrades don't want any mixing with whites. They
have ordered that contact must be kept at a minimum.

ISABEL: And you go along with that.

THAMI: Yes.

ISABEL: Happily!

THAMI (*Goaded by her lack of understanding*): Yes! I go along happily with that!!

ISABEL: Hell, Thami, this great Beginning of yours sounds like . . . (*Shakes her head*) I don't know. Other people deciding who can and who can't be your friends, what you must do and what you can't do. Is this the Freedom you've been talking to me about? That you were going to fight for?

Mr. M enters quietly. His stillness is in disturbing contrast to the bustle and energy we have come to associate with him.

MR. M: Don't let me interrupt you. Please carry on. (*To Thami*) I'm most interested in your reply to that question. (*Pause*) I think he's forgotten what it was Isabel. Ask him again.

ISABEL (*Backing out of the confrontation*): No. Forget it.

MR. M (*Persisting*): Isabel was asking you how you managed to reconcile your desire for Freedom with what the Comrades are doing.

ISABEL: I said forget it Mr. M. I'm not interested anymore.

MR. M (*Insistent*): But I am.

THAMI: The Comrades are imposing a discipline which our struggle needs at this point. There is no comparison between that and the total denial of our Freedom by the white government. They have been forcing on us an inferior education in order to keep us permanently suppressed. When our struggle is successful there will be no more need for the discipline the Comrades are demanding.

MR. M (*Grudging admiration*): Oh Thami . . . you learn your lessons so well! The "revolution" has only just begun and you are already word perfect. So then tell me, do you

think I agree with this inferior "Bantu Education" that is
being forced on you?

THAMI: You teach it.

MR. M: But unhappily so! Most unhappily, unhappily so!
Don't you know that? Did you have your fingers in your
ears the thousand times I've said so in the classroom?
Where were you when I stood there and said I regarded it
as my duty, my deepest obligation to you young men and
women to sabotage it, and that my conscience would not
let me rest until I had succeeded. And I have! Yes, I have
succeeded! I have got irrefutable proof of my success. You!
Yes. You can stand here and accuse me, unjustly, because I
have also had a struggle and I have won mine. I have
liberated your mind in spite of what the Bantu Education
was trying to do to it. Your mouthful of big words and
long sentences which the not-so-clever Comrades are
asking you to speak and write for them, your wonderful
eloquence at last night's meeting which got them all so
excited—yes, I heard about it!—you must thank me for
all of that, Thami.

THAMI: No I don't. You never taught me those lessons.

MR. M: Oh I see. You have got other teachers have you?

THAMI: Yes. Yours were lessons in whispering. There are men
now who are teaching us to shout. Those little tricks and
jokes of yours in the classroom liberated nothing. The
struggle doesn't need the big English words you taught
me how to spell.

MR. M: Be careful, Thami. Be careful! Be careful! Don't scorn
words. They are sacred! Magical! Yes, they are. Do you
know that without words a man can't think? Yes, it's true.
Take that thought back with you as a present from the
despised Mr. M and share it with the Comrades. Tell
them the difference between a man and an animal is that
Man thinks, and he thinks with words. Consider the

58

mighty ox. Four powerful legs, massive shoulders, and a
beautiful thick hide that gave our warriors shields to
protect them when they went into battle. Think of his
beautiful head, Thami, the long horns, the terrible bellow
from his lungs when he charges a rival! *But it has got no
words and therefore it is stupid!* And along comes that funny
little hairless animal that has got only two thin legs, no
horns and a skin worth nothing and he tells that ox what
to do. He is its master and he is that because he can
speak! If the struggle needs weapons give it words Thami.
Stones and petrol bombs can't get inside those armored
cars. Words can. They can do something even more
devastating than that . . . they can get inside the heads of
those inside the armored cars. I speak to you like this
because if I have faith in anything, it is faith in the power
of the word. Like my master, the great Confucius, I
believe that, using only words, a man can right a wrong
and judge and execute the wrongdoer. You are meant to
use words like that.

Talk to others. Bring them back into the classroom.
They will listen to you. They look up to you as a leader.

THAMI: No I won't. You talk about them as if they were a lot
of sheep waiting to be led. They know what they are
doing. They'd call me a traitor if I tried to persuade them
otherwise.

MR. M: Then listen carefully Thami. I have received
instructions from the department to make a list of all
those who take part in the boycott. Do you know what
they will do with that list when all this is over . . .
because don't fool yourself Thami, it will be. When your
boycott comes to an inglorious end like all the others . . .
they will make all of you apply for readmission and if your
name is on that list . . . *(He leaves the rest unspoken)*

THAMI: Will you do it? Will you make that list for them?

MR. M: That is none of your business.

THAMI: Then don't ask me questions about mine.

MR. M *(His control finally snaps. He explodes with anger and bitterness)*: Yes, I will! I will ask you all the questions I like. And you know why? Because I am a man and you are a boy. And if you are not in that classroom tomorrow you will be a very, very silly boy.

THAMI: Then don't call me names, Mr. M.

MR. M: No? Then what must I call you? Comrade Thami? Never! You are a silly boy now, and without an education you will grow up to be a stupid man!

For a moment it looks as if Thami is going to leave without saying anything more, but he changes his mind and confronts Mr. M for the last time.

THAMI: The others called *you* names at the meeting last night. Did your spies tell you that? Government stooge, sellout, collaborator. They said you licked the white man's arse and would even eat his shit if it meant keeping your job. Did your spies tell you that I tried to stop them saying those things? Don't wait until tomorrow to make your list Mr. M. You can start now. Write down the first name: Thami Mbikwana.

He leaves. A few seconds of silence after Thami's departure. Isabel makes a move towards Mr. M, but he raises his hand sharply, stopping her, keeping her at a distance.

ISABEL: This fucking country! *(She leaves)*

SCENE 2

Mr. M alone. His mood at the beginning of the scene is one of quiet, vacant disbelief.

MR. M: It was like being in a nightmare. I was trying to get
to the school, I knew that if I didn't hurry I was going to
be late so I *had to get to the school* . . . but every road I
took was blocked by policemen and soldiers with their
guns ready, or Comrades building barricades. First I tried
Jabulani Street, then I turned into Kwaza Road and then
Lamini Street . . . and then I gave up and just wandered
around aimlessly, helplessly, watching my world go mad
and set itself on fire. Everywhere I went . . . overturned
buses, looted bread vans, the government offices . . .
everything burning and the children dancing around
rattling boxes of matches and shouting *"Tshisa! Qhumisa!*
Tshisa! Qhumisa! Qhumisa!" . . . and then running for
their lives when the police armored cars appeared. They
were everywhere, crawling around in the smoke like giant
dung beetles looking for shit to eat.

I ended up on the corner where Mrs. Makatini always
sits selling *vetkoek* and prickly pears to people waiting for
the bus. The only person there was little Sipho Fondini
from Standard Six, writing on the wall: "Liberation First,
then Education." He saw me and he called out: "Is the
spelling right Mr. M?" And he meant it! The young eyes
in that smoke-stained little face were terribly serious.

Somewhere else a police van raced past me crowded
with children who should have also been in their desks in
school. Their hands waved desperately through the bars,
their voices called out: "Teacher! Teacher! Help us! Tell
our mothers. Tell our fathers." "No Anela," I said. "This
is too much now. Just stand here and close your eyes and
wait until you wake up and find your world the way it
was." But that didn't happen. A police car came around
the corner and suddenly there were children everywhere
throwing stones and tear-gas bombs falling all around and
I knew that I wasn't dreaming, that I was coughing and

choking and hanging on to a lamppost in the real world.
No! No!

Do something Anela. Do something. Stop the madness!
Stop the madness.

SCENE 3

*Mr. M alone in Number One Classroom. He is ringing his school
bell wildly.*

MR. M: Come to school! Come to school. Before they kill you
all, come to school!

*Silence. Mr. M looks around the empty classroom. He goes to his
table, and after composing himself, opens the class register and
reads out the names as he does every morning at the start of a
new school day.*

Johnny Awu, living or dead? Christopher Bandla, living or
dead? Zandile Cwati, living or dead? Semphiwe Dambuza
. . . Ronald Gxasheka . . . Noloyiso Mfundweni . . .
Steven Gaika . . . Zachariah Jabavu . . . Thami . . .
Thami Mbikwana . . .

(Pause) Living or dead?

How many young souls do I have present this morning?
There are a lot of well-aimed stray bullets flying around on
the streets out there. Is that why this silence is so . . .
heavy?

But what can I teach you? *(Picks up his little black
dictionary on the table)* My lessons were meant to help you
in *this* world. I wanted you to know how to read and write
and talk in *this* world of living, stupid, cruel men.

(Helpless gesture) Now? Oh my children! I have no
lessons that will be of any use to you now. Mr. M and all
of his wonderful words are . . . useless, useless, useless!

The sound of breaking glass. Stones land in the classroom. Mr. M picks up one.

No! One of you is still alive. Ghosts don't throw stones with hot, sweating young hands. *(Grabs the bell and rings it wildly again)* Come to school! Come to school!

Thami appears.

THAMI *(Quietly)*: Stop ringing that bell, Mr. M.

MR. M: Why? It's only the school bell, Thami. I thought you liked the sound of it. You once told me it was almost as good as music . . . don't you remember?

THAMI: You are provoking the Comrades with it.

MR. M: No Thami. I am summoning the Comrades with it.

THAMI: They say you are ringing the bell to taunt them. You are openly defying the boycott by being here in the school.

MR. M: I ring this bell because according to my watch it is schooltime and I am a teacher and those desks are empty! I will go on ringing it as I have been doing these past two weeks, at the end of every lesson. And you can tell the Comrades that I will be back here ringing it tomorrow and the day after tomorrow and for as many days after that as it takes for this world to come to its senses.

Is that the only reason you've come? To tell me to stop ringing the school bell?

THAMI: No.

MR. M: You haven't come for a lesson have you?

THAMI: No I haven't.

MR. M: Of course not. What's the matter with me. Slogans don't need much in the way of grammar do they. As for these . . . *(The stone in his hand)* No, you don't need me for lessons in stone-throwing either. You've already got teachers in those very revolutionary subjects haven't you.

(Picks up his dictionary. The stone in one hand, the book in

63

the other) You know something interesting, Thami . . . if
you put these two on a scale I think you would find that
they weighed just about the same. But in this hand I am,
holding the whole English language. This . . . *(The stone)*
is just *one* word in that language. It's true! All that
wonderful poetry that you and Isabel tried to cram into
your beautiful heads . . . in here! Twenty-six letters, sixty
thousand words. The greatest souls the world has ever
known were able to open the floodgates of their ecstasy,
their despair, their joy! . . . with the words in this little
book! Aren't you tempted? I was.

(*Opens the book at the flyleaf and reads)* "Anela Myalatya.
Cookhouse. 1947." One of the first books I ever bought.
(Impulsively) I want you to have it.

THAMI *(Ignoring the offered book)*: I've come here to warn you.

MR. M: You've already done that and I've already told you that
you are wasting your breath. Now take your stones and
go. There are a lot of unbroken windows left.

THAMI: I'm not talking about the bell now. It's more serious
than that.

MR. M: In my life nothing is more serious than ringing the
school bell.

THAMI: There was a meeting last night. Somebody stood up
and denounced you as an informer.

Pause. Thami waits. Mr. M says nothing.

He said you gave names to the police.

Mr. M says nothing.

Everybody is talking about it this morning. You are in
big danger.

MR. M: Why are you telling me all this?

THAMI: So that you can save yourself. There's a plan to march
to the school and burn it down. If they find you here . . .

64

Pause.

MR. M: Go on. *(Violently)* If they find me here *what?*

THAMI: They will kill you.

MR. M: "They will kill me." That's better. Remember what I
taught you . . . if you've got a problem, put it into words so
that you can look at it, handle it, and ultimately solve it.
They will kill me! You are right. That is very serious. So then
. . . what must I do? Must I run away and hide somewhere?

THAMI: No, they will find you. You must join the boycott.

MR. M: I'm listening.

THAMI: Let me go back and tell them that we have had a long
talk and that you have realized you were wrong and have
decided to join us. Let me say that you will sign the
declaration and that you won't have anything to do with
the school until all demands have been met.

MR. M: And they will agree to that? Accept me as one of
them even though it is believed that I am an informer?

THAMI: I will tell them you are innocent. That I confronted
you with the charge and that you denied it and that I
believe you.

MR. M: I see. *(Studying Thami intently)* You don't believe that I
am an informer.

THAMI: No.

MR. M: Won't you be taking a chance in defending me like
that? Mightn't they end up suspecting you?

THAMI: They'll believe me. I'll make them believe me.

MR. M: You can't be sure. Mobs don't listen to reason Thami.
Hasn't your revolution already taught you that? Why take
a chance like that to save a collaborator? Why do you want
to do all this for me?

THAMI *(Avoiding Mr. M's eyes)*: I'm not doing it for you. I'm
doing it for the Struggle. Our Cause will suffer if we
falsely accuse and hurt innocent people.

MR. M: I see. My "execution" would be an embarrassment to the Cause. I apologize Thami. For a moment I allowed myself to think that you were doing it because we were . . . who we are . . . the "all-knowing Mr. M and his brilliant protégé Thami"! I was so proud of us when Isabel called us that.

Well young Comrade, you have got nothing to worry about. Let them come and do whatever it is they want to. Your Cause won't be embarrassed, because you see, they won't be "hurting" an innocent man.

(He makes his confession simply and truthfully) That's right Thami. I am guilty. I did go to the police. I sat down in Captain Lategan's office and told him I felt it was my duty to report the presence in our community of strangers from the north. I told him that I had reason to believe that they were behind the present unrest. I gave the Captain names and addresses. He thanked me and offered me money for the information—which I refused.

(Pause) Why do you look at me like that? Isn't that what you expected from me? . . . a government stooge, a sellout, an arse-licker? Isn't that what you were all secretly hoping I would do . . . so that you could be proved right? *(Appalled)* Is that why I did it? Out of spite? Can a man destroy himself, his life for a reason as petty as that?

I sat here before going to the police station saying to myself that it was my duty, to my conscience, to you, to the whole community to do whatever I could to put an end to this madness of boycotts and arson, mob violence and lawlessness . . . and maybe that is true . . . but only maybe . . . because Thami, the truth is that I was so lonely! You had deserted me. I was so jealous of those who had taken you away. *Now,* I've *really* lost you, haven't I? Yes. I can see it in your eyes. You'll never forgive me for doing that, will you?

You know Thami, I'd sell my soul to have you all back
behind your desks for one last lesson. Yes. If the devil
thought it was worth having and offered me that in
exchange—one lesson!—he could have my soul. So then
it's all over! Because this . . . *(The classroom)* is all there
was for me. This was my home, my life, my one and only
ambition . . . to be a good teacher! *(His dictionary)* Anela
Myalatya, twenty years old, from Cookhouse, wanted to be
that the way your friends wanted to be big soccer stars
playing for Kaizer Chiefs! That ambition goes back to
when he was just a skinny little ten-year-old pissing on a
small gray bush at the top of the Wapadsberg Pass.

We were on our way to a rugby match at Somerset
East. The lorry stopped at the top of the mountain so that
we could stretch our legs and relieve ourselves. It was a
hard ride on the back of that lorry. The road hadn't been
tarred yet. So there I was, ten years old and sighing with
relief as I aimed for the little bush. It was a hot day. The
sun right over our heads . . . not a cloud in the vast blue
sky. I looked out . . . it's very high up there at the top of
the pass . . . and there it was, stretching away from the
foot of the mountain, the great pan of the Karoo . . .
stretching away forever it seemed into the purple haze and
heat of the horizon. Something grabbed my heart at that
moment, my soul, and squeezed it until there were tears
in my eyes. I had never seen anything so big, so beautiful
in all my life. I went to the teacher who was with us and
asked him: "Teacher, where will I come to if I start
walking that way?" . . . and I pointed. He laughed.
"Little man," he said, "that way is north. If you start
walking that way and just keep on walking, and your legs
don't give in, you will see all of Africa! Yes, Africa little
man! You will see the great rivers of the continent: the
Vaal, the Zambesi, the Limpopo, the Congo and then the

mighty Nile. You will see the mountains: the
Drakensberg, Kilimanjaro, Kenya and the Ruwenzori.
And you will meet all our brothers: the little Pygmies of
the forests, the proud Masai, the Watusi . . . tallest of the
tall and the Kikuyu standing on one leg like herons in a
pond waiting for a frog." "Has teacher seen all that?" I
asked. "No," he said. "Then how does teacher know it's
there?" "Because it is all in the books and I have read the
books and if you work hard in school little man, you can
do the same without worrying about your legs giving in."

He was right Thami. *I* have seen it. It is all there in
the books just as he said it was and I have made it mine. I
can stand on the banks of all those great rivers, look up at
the majesty of all those mountains, whenever I want to. It
is a journey I have made many times. Whenever my spirit
was low and I sat alone in my room, I said to myself:
Walk Anela! Walk! . . . and I imagined myself at the foot
of the Wapadsberg setting off for that horizon that called
me that day forty years ago. It always worked! When I left
that little room, I walked back into the world a proud
man, because I was an African and all the splendor was
my birthright.

(Pause) I don't want to make that journey again Thami.
There is someone waiting for me now at the end of it who
has made a mockery of all my visions of splendor. He has
in his arms my real birthright. I saw him on the
television in the Reverend Mbopa's lounge. An Ethopian
tribesman, and he was carrying the body of a little child
that had died of hunger in the famine . . . a small bundle
carelessly wrapped in a few rags. I couldn't tell how old
the man was. The lines of despair and starvation on his
face made him look as old as Africa itself.

He held that little bundle very lightly as he shuffled
along to a mass grave, and when he reached it, he didn't

have the strength to kneel and lay it down gently. . . . He just opened his arms and let it fall. I was very upset when the program ended. Nobody had thought to tell us his name and whether he was the child's father, or grandfather, or uncle. And the same for the baby! Didn't it have a name? How dare you show me one of our children being thrown away and not tell me its name! I demand to know who is in that bundle!

(Pause) Not knowing their names doesn't matter anymore. They are more than just themselves. The tribesmen and dead child do duty for all of us Thami. Every African soul is either carrying that bundle or in it.

What is wrong with this world that it wants to waste you all like that . . . my children . . . my Africa!

(Holding out a hand as if he wanted to touch Thami's face) My beautiful and proud young Africa!

More breaking glass and stones and the sound of a crowd outside the school. Mr. M starts to move. Thami stops him.

THAMI: No! Don't go out there. Let me speak to them first. Listen to me! I will tell them I have confronted you with the charges and that you have denied them and that I believe you. I will tell them you are innocent.

MR. M: You will lie for me, Thami?

THAMI: Yes.

MR. M *(Desperate to hear the truth)*: Why?

Thami can't speak.

Why will you lie for me Thami?

THAMI: I've told you before.

MR. M: The "Cause"?

THAMI: Yes.

MR. M: Then I do not need to hide behind your lies.

THAMI: They will kill you.

MR. M: Do you think I'm frightened of them? Do you think
I'm frightened of dying?

*Mr. M breaks away from Thami. Ringing his bell furiously he
goes outside and confronts the mob. They kill him.*

SCENE 4

Thami waiting. Isabel arrives.

THAMI: Isabel.

ISABEL *(It takes her a few seconds to respond):* Hello Thami.

THAMI: Thank you for coming.

ISABEL *(She is tense. Talking to him is not easy):* I wasn't going
to. Let me tell you straight out that there is nothing in
this world . . . nothing! . . . that I want to see less at
this moment than anything or anybody from the location.
But you said in your note that it was urgent, so here I
am. If you've got something to say, I'll listen.

THAMI: Are you in a hurry?

ISABEL: I haven't got to be somewhere else, if that's what you
mean. But if you're asking because it looks as if I would
like to run away from here, from you!—very fast—then
the answer is yes. But don't worry I'll be able to control
that urge for as long as you need to say what you want to.

THAMI *(Awkward in the face of Isabel's severe and unyielding
attitude):* I just wanted to say good-bye.

ISABEL: Again?

THAMI: What do you mean?

ISABEL: You've already done that Thami. Maybe you didn't use
that word, but you turned your back on me and walked
out of my life that last afternoon the three of us . . . *(She
can't finish)* How long ago was that?

THAMI: Three weeks I think.

ISABEL: So why do you want to do it again? Aren't you happy with the last time? It was so dramatic Thami!

THAMI *(Patiently)*: I wanted to see you because I'm leaving the town, I'm going away for good.

ISABEL: Oh I see. This is meant to be a "sad" good-bye is it? *(She is on the edge)* I'm sorry if I'm hurting your feelings but I thought you wanted to see me because you had something to say about recent events in our little community . . . *(She takes a crumpled little piece of newspaper out of her pocket and opens it with unsteady hands)* a certain unrest-related . . . I think that is the phrase they use . . . yes . . . here it is . . . *(Reading)* ". . . unrest-related incident in which according to witnesses the defenseless teacher was attacked by a group of blacks who struck him over the head with an iron rod before setting him on fire."

THAMI: Stop it Isabel.

ISABEL *(Fighting hard for self-control)*: Oh Thami, I wish I could! I've tried everything, but nothing helps. It just keeps going around and around inside my head. I've tried crying. I've tried praying! I've even tried confrontation. *Ja*, the day after it happened I tried to get into the location. I wanted to find the witnesses who reported it so accurately and ask them: "Why didn't you stop it!" There was a police roadblock at the entrance and they wouldn't let me in. They thought I was crazy or something and "escorted" me back into the safekeeping of two now very frightened parents.

There is nothing wrong with me! All I need is someone to tell me why he was killed. What madness drove those people to kill a man who had devoted his whole life to helping them. He was such a good man Thami! He was one of the most beautiful human beings I have ever known and his death is one of the ugliest things I have ever known.

Thami gives her a few seconds to calm down.

THAMI *(Gently)*: He was an informer Isabel. Somehow or the other somebody discovered that Mr. M was an informer.

ISABEL: You mean that list of pupils taking part in the boycott? You call that informing?

THAMI: No. It was worse than that. He went to the police and gave them the names and addresses of our political action committee. All of them were arrested after his visit. They are now in detention.

ISABEL: Mr. M did that?

THAMI: Yes.

ISABEL: I don't believe it.

THAMI: It's true Isabel.

ISABEL: No! What proof do you have?

THAMI: His own words. He told me so himself. I didn't believe it either when he was first accused, but the last time I saw him, he said it was true, that he had been to the police.

ISABEL *(Stunned disbelief)*: Mr. M? A police spy? For how long?

THAMI: No. It wasn't like that. He wasn't paid or anything. He went to the police just that one time. He said he felt it was his duty.

ISABEL: And what do you mean?

THAMI: Operation Qhumisa . . . the boycotts and strikes, the arson . . . you know he didn't agree with any of that. But he was also very confused about it all. I think he wished he had never done it.

ISABEL: So he went to the police just once.

THAMI: Yes.

ISABEL: As a matter of conscience.

THAMI: Yes.

ISABEL: That doesn't make him an "informer" Thami!

THAMI: Then what do you call somebody who gives information to the police?

ISABEL: No! You know what that word really means, the sort of person it suggests. Was Mr. M one of those? He was acting out of concern for his people . . . you said so yourself. He thought he was doing the right thing! You don't murder a man for that!

THAMI (*Near the end of his patience*): Be careful Isabel.

ISABEL: Of what?

THAMI: The words you use.

ISABEL: Oh? Which one don't you like? Murder? What do you want me to call it . . . "an unrest-related incident"? If you are going to call him an informer, then I am going to call his death murder!

THAMI: It was an act of self-defense.

ISABEL: By whom?

THAMI: The People.

ISABEL (*Almost speechless with outrage*): What? A mad mob attacks one unarmed defenseless man and you want me to call it—

THAMI (*Abandoning all attempts at patience. He speaks with the full authority of the anger inside him*): Stop Isabel! You just keep quiet now and listen to me. You're always saying you want to understand us and what it means to be black . . . well if you do, listen to me carefully now. I don't call it murder, and I don't call the people who did it a mad mob and yes, I do expect you to see it as an act of self-defense—listen to me!—blind and stupid but still self-defense.

He betrayed us and our fight for freedom. Five men are in detention because of Mr. M's visit to the police station. There have been other arrests and there will be more. Why do you think I'm running away?

How were those people to know he wasn't a paid informer who had been doing it for a long time and would do it again? They were defending themselves against what they thought was a terrible danger to themselves. What Anela Myalatya did to them and their cause is what your laws define as treason when it is done to you and threatens the safety and security of your comfortable white world. Anybody accused of it is put on trial in your courts and if found guilty they get hanged. Many of my people have been found guilty and have been hanged. Those hangings *we* call murder!

Try to understand, Isabel. Try to imagine what it is like to be a black person, choking inside with rage and frustration, bitterness, and then to discover that one of your own kind is a traitor, has betrayed you to those responsible for the suffering and misery of your family, of your people. What would you do? Remember there is no magistrate or court you can drag him to and demand that he be tried for that crime. There is no justice for black people in this country other than what we make for ourselves. When you judge us for what happened in front of the school four days ago just remember that you carry a share of the responsibility for it. It is your laws that have made simple, decent black people so desperate that they turn into "mad mobs."

Isabel has been listening and watching intently. It looks as if she is going to say something but she stops herself.

Say it, Isabel.

ISABEL: No.

THAMI: This is your last chance. You once challenged me to be honest with you. I'm challenging you now.

ISABEL *(She faces him)*: Where were you when it happened Thami? *(Pause)* And if you were, did you try to stop them?

THAMI: Isn't there a third question Isabel? Was I one of the mob that killed him?

ISABEL: Yes. Forgive me, Thami—please forgive me!—but there is that question as well Only once! Believe me, only once—late at night when I couldn't sleep. I couldn't believe it was there in my head, but I heard the words: "Was Thami one of the ones who did it?"

THAMI: If the police catch me, that's the question they will ask.

ISABEL: I'm asking you because . . . *(An open, helpless gesture)* I'm lost! I don't know what to think or feel anymore. Help me. Please. You're the only one who can. Nobody else seems to understand that I loved him.

This final confrontation is steady and unflinching on both sides.

THAMI: Yes, I was there. Yes, I did try to stop it. *(He gives Isabel the time to deal with this answer)* I knew how angry the people were. I went to warn him. If he had listened to me he would still be alive, but he wouldn't. It was almost as if he wanted it to happen. I think he hated himself very much for what he had done Isabel. He kept saying to me that it was all over. He was right. There was nothing left for him. That visit to the police station had finished everything. Nobody would have ever spoken to him again or let him teach their children.

ISABEL: Oh Thami, it is all so wrong! So stupid! That's what I can't take . . . the terrible stupidity of it. We needed him. All of us.

THAMI: I know.

ISABEL: Then why is he dead?

THAMI: You must stop asking these questions Isabel. You know the answers.

ISABEL: They don't make any sense Thami.

THAMI: I know what you are feeling. *(Pause)* I also loved him. Doesn't help much to say it now I know, but I did.

Because he made me angry and impatient with his "old-fashioned" ideas, I didn't want to admit it. Even if I had, it wouldn't have stopped me from doing what I did, the boycott and everything, but I should have tried harder to make him understand why I was doing it. You were right to ask about that. Now . . . ? *(A helpless gesture)* You know the most terrible words in your language, Isabel? Too late.

ISABEL: *Ja.*

THAMI: I'll never forgive myself for not trying harder with him and letting him know . . . my true feelings for him. Right until the end I tried to deny it . . . to him, to myself.

ISABEL: I'm sorry. I . . .

THAMI: That's all right.

ISABEL: Are the police really looking for you?

THAMI: Yes. Some of my friends have already been detained. They're pulling in anybody they can get their hands on.

ISABEL: Where are you going? Cape Town?

THAMI: No. That's the first place they'll look. I've written to my parents telling them about everything. I'm heading north.

ISABEL: To where?

THAMI: Far Isabel. I'm leaving the country.

ISABEL: Does that mean what I think it does?

THAMI *(He nods)*: I'm going to join the movement. I want to be a fighter. I've been thinking about it for a long time. Now I know it's the right thing to do. I don't want to end up being one of the mob that killed Mr. M—but that will happen to me if I stay here.

ISABEL: Oh, Thami.

THAMI: I know I'm doing the right thing. Believe me.

ISABEL: I'll try.

THAMI: And you?

ISABEL: I don't know what to do with myself Thami. All I
know is that I'm frightened of losing him. He's only been
dead four days and I think I'm already starting to forget
what he looked like. But the worst thing is that there's
nowhere for me to go and . . . you know . . . just be near
him. That's so awful. I got my father to phone the police
but they said there wasn't enough left of him to justify a
grave. What there was has been disposed of in a
"Christian manner." So where do I go? The burnt-out
ruins of the school? I couldn't face that.

THAMI: Get your father or somebody to drive you to the top
of the Wapadsberg Pass. It's on the road to Craddock.

ISABEL: I know it.

THAMI: It was a very special place to him. He told me that it
was there where it all started, where he knew what he
wanted to do with his life . . . being a teacher, being the
Mr. M we knew. You'll be near him up there. I must go
now.

ISABEL: Do you need any money?

THAMI: No. *Sala Kakuhle* Isabel. That's the Xhosa good-bye.

ISABEL: I know it. U'sispumla taught me how to say it.
Hamba Kakuhle Thami.

Thami leaves.

SCENE 5

*Isabel alone. She stands quietly, examining the silence. After a
few seconds she nods her head slowly.*

ISABEL: Yes! Thami was right Mr. M. He said I'd feel near
you up here.

He's out there somewhere Mr. M . . . traveling north.
He didn't say where exactly he was going, but I think we

can guess, can't we.

I'm here for a very "old-fashioned" reason, so I know you'll approve. I've come to pay my last respects to Anela Myalatya. I know the old-fashioned way of doing that is to bring flowers, lay them on the grave, say a quiet prayer and then go back to your life. But that seemed sort of silly this time. You'll have enough flowers around here when the spring comes . . . which it will. So instead I've brought you something which I know will mean more to you than flowers or prayers ever could. A promise. I am going to make Anela Myalatya a promise.

You gave me a little lecture once about wasted lives . . . how much of it you'd seen, how much you hated it, how much you didn't want that to happen to Thami and me. I sort of understood what you meant at the time. Now, I most certainly do. Your death has seen to that.

My promise to you is that I am going to try as hard as I can, in every way that I can, to see that it doesn't happen to me. I am going to try my best to make my life useful in the way yours was. I want you to be proud of me. After all, I am one of your children you know. You did welcome me to your family.

(A pause) The future is still ours, Mr. M.

The actor leaves the stage.

END OF PLAY